The Transformation Playbook

How To Achieve Success and Avoid Failure

Best Practice Guides for Best Practices To Planning,
Transformation, Technology, and Innovation.

Ken Martin

Copyright

Copyright © 2023 by 3 Magic Publications

All rights reserved. No part of this book may be reproduced, stored in a retrieval system or transmitted, in any form or by any means, without the prior written consent of the publisher, except in the case of brief quotations, embodied in reviews and articles. All third-party copyrights are acknowledged.

Although the author and publisher have made every effort to ensure that the information in this book is correct at press time, the author and publisher do not assume or hereby disclaim any liability to any party for any loss, damage, or disruption caused by errors or omissions, whether such errors or omissions result from negligence, accident, or any other cause.

Dedication

This book is dedicated to my amazing twin boys Jack and Jake.

Content

Copyright	2
Dedication	3
Content	4
Preface	7
Introduction	10
The One Page Planning Process	11
One Page Plan Linkages	12
The Master Program Plan	13
1.0 Vision Workstream Plan	14
2.0 People Workstream Plan	15
3.0 Process Workstream Plan	16
4.0 Technology Workstream Plan	17
5.0 Governance Workstream Plan	18
The Master Plan	20
The Master Program Plan	21
1.0 Vision	31
1.0 Vision Plan Linkages	32
1.0 Vision Workstream Plan	33
1.1 Strategy	34
1.2 Leadership	42
1.3 Roadmap	50
1.4 Agile PMO	59
1.5 Resources	69
2.0 People	79
2.0 People Plan Linkages	80
2.0 People Workstream Plan	81
2.1 Leadership	82
2.2 Stakeholders	89

Content

- 2.3 Communications 97
- 2.4 Change Impact 104
- 2.5 Training 111
- 3.0 Process 119
  - 3.0 Process Plan Linkages 120
  - 3.0 Process Workstream Plan 121
  - 3.1 CX Definition 122
  - 3.2 Process Analysis 129
  - 3.3 Process Testing 137
  - 3.4 Process Application 144
  - 3.5 Process Metrics 151
- 4.0 Technology 158
  - 4.0 Technology Plan Linkages 159
  - 4.0 Technology Workstream Plan 160
  - 4.1 Technology Team 161
  - 4.2 ASIS Infrastructure 170
  - 4.3 Tech innovation 177
  - 4.4 Tech application 185
  - 4.5 Technology Metrics 192
- 5.0 Governance 200
  - 5.0 Governance Plan Linkages 201
  - 5.0 Governance Workstream Plan 202
  - 5.1 Steering Group 203
  - 5.2 Framework 210
  - 5.3 PMO Govern 217
  - 5.4 Program Plan 224
  - 5.5 Change & Comms 231
- Acknowledgements 246
- 3 Magic Publications 247

CONSIDER HOW HARD IT IS TO CHANGE YOURSELF AND YOU'LL UNDERSTAND WHAT LITTLE CHANCE YOU HAVE IN TRYING TO.

Benjamin Franklin

Preface

I have always been interested in effective communications and the art of making the complex simple. This approach is the primary goal of 3 Magic Publications, which I have founded to facilitate successful business change and transformation by using innovative and creative documentation to communicate key messages and best practices.

During my career, I wanted a reference method of best practices at my fingertips, where, instead of reading numerous self-development, management, and technical books, I could have a handy one-page cheat sheet. So, I developed the "One Page Magic" – the idea of having one book on a page which has evolved into this new table format. I hope you find these best practice guides useful for your continued success in your career.

Ken Martin

THE ONLY THING THAT IS CONSTANT IS CHANGE.

Heraclitus

The Transformation Playbook

Introduction

How to read

The Transformation Playbook comprises hands-on experience and best practices that cover all aspects of planning, implementing and risk management for successful organizational change management projects.

Why use best practices?

There is a well-known phrase - "Keep doing the same things and expecting different results is a sign of insanity". Yet this is what many people and companies continue to do by doing the same things, making the same mistakes, and expecting different results. But how many professionals have recorded lessons learned and even more rarely how many professionals have read lessons learned from other's experiences of previous projects?

Best practices often derived from lessons learned and hard-earned experience can save you a lot of wasted effort, time, and often failure. They can contribute to your success in all aspects of your career and life. Learn from others' best practices experiences and avoid common mistakes and succeed for the first time.

The One Page Planning Process

A vision for the firm will be realised with the aid of a defined strategy that will guide the creation of a detailed transformation plan.

The one-page planning is a simple and effective planning & governance process.

Once this simple process is set up it is very effective, it continually shows the big picture, highlights accountability and gains engagement and buy-in from the teams and stakeholders.

The business transformation program's workstreams (subprojects) are all listed in the one-page master plan, which also specifies the changes that must be implemented and when. Each workstream needs to have specific goals, benchmarks, parameters, timetables, and financial constraints.

One Page Planning Linkages:
This diagram on the next page shows the linkages between the master one-page plan and a work-stream one page plan with clear accountabilities.

The Master One Page Plan
The Master One Page Plan provides an overview of all work-streams for reporting with a PM assigned as owner to each work stream.

The Workstream One Page Plans:
The workstream one page plans feed into the master one-page plan as supporting workstreams. Work-stream support plans are typically owned by a PM but the work-streams in those work-stream plans can be assigned owners to SMEs and stakeholders.

Change is difficult...

Implementing change within an organisation can be a very difficult task. People don't alter their characteristics or how they perceive the world just because a change project is imminent.

Having the right people with the right skill sets and an effective organisational change management plan are both critical success factors for a business transformation.

One Page Plan Linkages

The Master Program Plan

Business Transformation - Master

Sponsor	O. Twist
Program Mgr.	B. Sykes
Completion Date	15th Feb 2024
Overall Status	Green

Goal: A successful business transformation with a seamless implementation & high user adoption where all stakeholders support and are engaged delivering all the desired business benefits, outcomes and improved customer experience (CX).

Workstream Outcomes

Key Areas						Outcomes
Vision	**Strategy** – The current and future business strategy (goals and outcomes)	**Leadership** – Appoint a PM & leaders to provide program support	**Roadmap** – Develop a detailed roadmap of changes and deliverables	**Agile Trans PMO** – Set up an agile trans PMO for transformation support & service	**Resources** – Choose the right skilled people to plan & implement program	A clear strategy with a supporting roadmap with a PM, a PMO & right skilled people
1.0 J. Smith	1.1 100 G	1.2 100 G	1.3 100 G	1.4 100 G	1.5 100 G	Status Green
People	**Leadership** – Leaders & sponsors aligned on success criteria & strategy	**Stakeholders** – All stakeholders are identified for impact & program support	**Communications** – The change is made visible & way to grow engagement	**Change impact** – The impact level is measured & plan for readiness developed	**Training** – The competencies required are built into the training plan	All stakeholders support and embrace the vision and are engaged to support it
2.0 L. Baine	2.1 100 G	2.2 100 G	2.3 100 G	2.4 100 G	2.5 100 G	Status Green
Process	**CX Definition** – Define the desired CX in current marketplace & client expectations	**Process Analysis** – Target processes to transform to meet business & CX goals	**Process Testing** – Test the processes for performance before going live	**Application** – Implement the new processes with new documentation	**Impact Metrics** – Measure the impact of the new processes & refine where required	All processes been transformed to meet business & CX goals
3.0 K. West	3.1 100 G	3.2 100 G	3.3 100 G	3.4 100 G	3.5 100 G	Status Green
Technology	**Tech Team** – Create a cross functional team to assess ASIS tech	**ASIS State** – Assess existing tools & software to identify gaps & opportunities	**Tech Innovation** – Assess new tech for TOBE infrastructure to aid transformation	**Tech Application** – Implement new tech to support business strategy and goals	**Tech Metrics** – Measure success of new technologies for transformation	Implement new TOBE infrastructure to support strategy goals & improved CX
4.0 P. Giles	4.1 100 G	4.2 100 G	4.3 100 G	4.4 100 G	4.5 100 G	Status Green
Governance	**Steering Group** – Define steering group for oversight & decision making	**Framework** – Create governance framework process for decision making	**PMO Govern** – Manage governance & progress at program levels	**Program Plan** – Review of program plans (progress, risks, schedule, budget)	**Change** – OCM & comms are proactively actioned & reported	Governance that aligns leadership & stakeholders with the change & program
5.0 B. Bass	5.1 100 G	5.2 100 G	5.3 100 G	5.4 100 G	5.5 100 G	Status Green

Status Labels: Workstream No. | % complete | Missed milestone, all status red, Going to miss milestone, status orange, All milestones met = Green

1.0 Vision Workstream Plan

Business Transformation: 1.0 Vision

Sponsor	O. Twist	
Program Mgr.	B. Sykes	
Completion	15th Feb 2024	
Overall Status	Green	

Goal: A clear strategy with a supporting roadmap with a PM, an agile PMO & right skilled people

Workstreams	Workstreams Activities					Outcomes
Strategy (1.1)	**Current Strategy** (1.11 / 100 / G) — Review the current and business strategy (goals and outcomes)	**Vision & goals** (1.12 / 100 / G) — Determine vision, goas, outcomes. tech, & processes for plan	**Roadmap** (1.13 / 100 / G) — Develop roadmap for program from the ASIS to TOBE state	**Deliverables** (1.14 / 100 / G) — Define the proposed deliverables of the transformation	**Metrics** (1.15 / 100 / G) — Identify metrics on how success will be measured	The current and future business strategy (goals and outcomes). Status: Green
Leadership (1.2)	**Program Mgr.** (1.21 / 100 / G) — Appoint program manager for the transformation	**Sponsor** (1.22 / 100 / G) — Appoint executive sponsor for the program	**Governance** (1.23 / 100 / G) — Create governance group of key leaders for the program	**Stakeholders** (1.24 / 100 / G) — Identify impacted stakeholders by the program	**PMO Leader** (1.25 / 100 / G) — Appoint PMO leader to lead & manager the transformation status	Appoint a PM & leaders to provide program support. Status: Green
Roadmap (1.3)	**ASIS Analysis** (1.31 / 100 / G) — Review ASIS systems & processes for improvements	**TOBE Design** (1.32 / 100 / G) — Identify gaps & create desired outcome for transformation	**Strategy Linkage** (1.33 / 100 / G) — Review proposed changes to strategic goals and ROI	**Goals** (1.34 / 100 / G) — Set clear, realistic, measurable goals for transformation	**Agile Approach** (1.35 / 100 / G) — Adopt an agile phased approach including OCM throughout	Develop a detailed roadmap of changes and deliverables. Status: Green
Agile Trans PMO (1.4)	**PMO Charter** (1.41 / 100 / G) — Create PMO charter that focuses on business value	**PMO Leader** (1.42 / 100 / G) — An agile PMO leader aligned to execution quality & transparency	**Lean Portfolio** (1.43 / 100 / G) — Program priorities aligned to value-add work streams & goals	**Enterprise Focus** (1.44 / 100 / G) — Delivery uses DevOps to coordinate work across streams	**Agile Delivery** (1.45 / 100 / G) — Agile project delivery used that begins with a customer focus	Set up an agile trans PMO for transformation support & service. Status: Green
Resources (1.5)	**Planning** (1.51 / 100 / G) — Determine resource needs: type, skills for the program	**Estimation** (1.52 / 100 / G) — How much time will each resource need for program delivery	**Acquisition** (1.53 / 100 / G) — Obtain resources (internally / externally) with right skills	**Agile Teams** (1.54 / 100 / G) — Create agile cross functional teams that are customer focused	**Evaluation** (1.55 / 100 / G) — Monitor & evaluate resources to meet program needs	Choose the right skilled people to plan & implement program. Status: Green

Status Labels: Workstream No. | % complete | Missed milestone, all status red, Going to miss milestone, status orange, All milestones met = Green

The Transformation Playbook

2.0 People Workstream Plan

Business Transformation: 2.0 People						Program Mgr.	Project Mgr.
						B. Sykes	L. Baines
Goal: All stakeholders support and embrace the vision and are engaged to support it.						Completion Date	Overall Status
						15th Feb 2024	Green

Leadership	**Mission** Communicate mission & vision to leaders & key stakeholders	**Engagement** Gather inputs from leaders & business for strategy plans	**Verification** Verify business goals and priorities after data gathering	**Strategic Plan** Create strategic plan to support business goals & priorities	**Comms Plan** Share plan for feedback and refinement	Leaders & sponsors aligned on success criteria and strategy
2.1	2.11 100 G	2.12 100 G	2.13 100 G	2.14 100 G	2.15 100 G	Status Green
Stakeholders	**Stakeholders** Identify the internal stakeholders (PM, team, sponsor)	**Suppliers** Identify the ext. stakeholders: users, suppliers, clients	**Charter** Use the program charter to identify & note stakeholders	**Meetings** Hold meetings to gain inputs & expectations, feedback & risks	**Comms** Document & share expectations, risks to all stakeholders	All stakeholders are identified for impact & program support
2.2	2.21 100 G	2.22 100 G	2.23 100 G	2.24 100 G	2.25 100 G	Status Green
Communications	**Assessment** Assess what's going to change, why and record the case for it	**Comms Plan** Create comms plan to inform & answer questions & concerns	**Influencers** Prepare leaders to communicate key change messages	**Comms Plan** Leaders convey consistent messages to meet staff needs	**Comms Metrics** Evaluate the result of comms on how staff are handling change	The change is made visible to grow engagement
2.3	2.31 100 G	2.32 100 G	2.33 100 G	2.34 100 G	2.35 100 G	Status Green
Change Impact	**ASIS State** Assess the current state before the proposed change	**TOBE State** Assess the future state after the proposed change	**Gap Analysis** Determine & validate impact between ASIS and TOBE states	**Transition** Sort transition needs based on impact & priority	**Decisions** Design decisions are based on identified impacts and needs	The impact level is measured & plan for readiness developed
2.4	2.41 100 G	2.42 100 G	2.43 100 G	2.44 100 G	2.45 100 G	Status Green
Training	**Assessment** Assessing needs and resources available to meet training needs	**Motivation** Identify incentives for leaders & staff to attend training	**Training Design** Plan training fit for purpose to the target audience	**Deliver Training** Clearly convey goals, objectives, and outcomes to learners	**Evaluation** Evaluation success of training and ides for improvement	The competencies required are built into the training plan
2.5	2.51 100 2.5	2.52 100 G	2.53 100 G	2.54 100 G	2.55 100 G	Status Green

Status Labels | Workstream No. | % complete | Missed milestone, all status red, Going to miss milestone, status orange, All milestones met = Green

15

3.0 Process Workstream Plan

Business Transformation: 3.0 Process

Goal: All processes been transformed to meet business & CX goals.

	Program Mgr.	Project Mgr.
	B. Sykes	K. West
	Completion Date	**Overall Status**
	15th Feb 2024	Green

3.1 CX Definition
Define the desired CX in current marketplace & client expectations

ID	Title	Description
3.11	Customer	Define ways for customers to be in control of content — 100 G
3.12	Relations	Tailor your product / services to customers (name, offers, loyalty) — 100 G
3.13	Omnichannel	Provide a seamless transition between platforms and devices — 100 G
3.14	CX Journey	Map out the customer journey and regularly update it — 100 G
3.15	Responsiveness	Be responsive to feedback & handle their issue effectively — 100 G

Status: Green

3.2 Process Analysis
Pinpoint processes to transform to meet business & CX goals

ID	Title	Description
3.21	Process Goals	Identify and define SMART goals for process analysis — 100 G
3.22	Processes	Identify processes and collect data on issues & bottlenecks — 100 G
3.23	Map Processes	Assemble team with process owners to map out process — 100 G
3.24	Analysis	Identify customer interactions, issues and bottlenecks — 100 G
3.25	Improvements	Identify opportunities to improve processes for automation & CX — 100 G

Status: Green

3.3 Process Testing
Test the processes to gauge performance before going live

ID	Title	Description
3.31	Testing Scope	Read & analyse the documents and requirements created — 100 G
3.32	Approach	Decide on testing approach & needs for testing the process — 100 G
3.33	Testing Tasks	Decide tasks to do in testing each phase of the process — 100 G
3.34	Testing Team	Define the role of testers and dates of the process tests — 100 G
3.35	Test Results	Review test results to see if process steps need refining — 100 G

Status: Green

3.4 Process Application
Implement the new processes with new documentation

ID	Title	Description
3.41	Review Goals	Review changes, documentation & goals of new process — 100 G
3.42	Determine Roles	Set expectations with uses & communicate implementation plan — 100 G
3.43	Delegation	Decide who needs to do what process tasks and when — 100 G
3.44	Execute Plan	Execute the plan, monitor progress and performance — 100 G
3.45	Adjust & Revise	Implementation is an iterative process so adjust when needed — 100 G

Status: Green

3.5 Process metrics
Measure the impact of the new processes & refine where required

ID	Title	Description
3.51	Primary Goals	Define primary goals for process success — 100 G
3.52	Metrics Selection	Choose appropriate metrics to measure — 100 G
3.53	Tools	Select tools and activities to capture selected metrics — 100 G
3.54	Record Metrics	Capture and record metrics — 100 G
3.55	Evaluation	Evaluate metrics against process goals — 100 G

Status: Green

Status Labels | Workstream No. | % complete | One red, then status red, One orange, then status orange, All green = Complete

4.0 Technology Workstream Plan

The Transformation Playbook

Business Transformation: 4.0 Technology						Program Mgr.	Project Mgr.
Goal: Implement new TOBE infrastructure to support strategy goals & improved CX						B. Sykes	P. Giles
						Completion Date	Overall Status
						15th Feb 2024	Green
Technology Team	**Business Arch.** Overseas design and execution of blueprint for the transformation	**Enterprise Arch.** EA oversee the design of IT orientated enterprise architecture	**Business Part.** Business SMEs and leaders who have inputs & influence	**Partners** Most firms require additional specialist skills and experience	**Other Functions** Other functions as IT departments and developers	Create a cross functional team to assess ASIS tech	
4.1	4.11 100 G	4.12 100 G	4.13 100 G	4.14 100 G	4.15 100 G	Status	Green
ASIS Infrastructure	**Backup /BC/DR** Take an inventory of the ASIS backup / BC/ DR environment	**Networks** Assess networks for robustness and performance	**Applications** Assess applications & servers to reduce costs & meet goals	**Storage** Assess storage and opportunities for virtualisation	**Gap Analysis** Perform a gap analysis of gaps to fix for transformation	Assess existing tools & software to identify gaps & opportunities	
4.2	4.21 100 G	4.22 100 G	4.23 100 G	4.24 100 G	4.25 100 G	Status	Green
Tech Innovation	**Cloud Services** Evaluate cloud as an enabler of speed, agility & resiliency	**AI** Assess the use of AI machine learning or for improved services	**Cybersecurity** Make cyber-security part of DNA with use of DevSecOps	**Automation** The use of RPA and other technologies to automate processes	**AI Governance** Build AI governance ethics into products for staff accountability	Assess new tech for TOBE infrastructure to aid transformation	
4.3	4.31 100 G	4.32 100 G	4.33 100 G	4.34 100 G	4.35 100 G	Status	Green
Tech Application	**Business Design** Review every element of the business model that affects the consumer experience	**Transformation** Map the "TOBE" customer journey to business capabilities & value add activities	**TOBE Tech** Design the "TOBE" infrastructure to deliver the business goals & capabilities	**Tech. Projects** Develop projects based on business requirements to deliver the capabilities	**Implementation** Use an agile process to implement tech to support new business processes and goals	Implement new TOBE infrastructure to support strategy goals & improved CX	
4.4	4.41 100 G	4.42 100 G	4.43 100 G	4.44 100 G	4.45 100 G	Status	Green
Technology Metrics	**IT Metrics** Align IT metrics with business goals & stakeholders	**Uptime** The amount of time that systems are available & functional	**MTTR Metrics** The mean time resolve, respond, repair, or recovery	**Customers** Understand business & customers & improve experience	**IT Metrics** IT metrics show the value of IT to the rest of the organization	Measure success of new technologies for transformation	
4.5	4.51 100 G	4.52 100 G	4.53 100 G	4.54 100 G	4.55 100 G	Status	Green

Status Labels | Workstream No. | % complete | One red, then status red, One orange, then status orange, All green = Complete

5.0 Governance Workstream Plan

Business Transformation: 5.0 Governance

					Program Mgr.	Project Mgr.
Goal: Governance that aligns leadership & stakeholders with the change & program					B. Sykes	B. Bass
					Completion	Overall Status
					15th Feb 2024	Green

Steering Group (5.1)

Executive Team	Sponsor(s)	Transformation	PM & PMO	IT/HR/Facility	
Ensure one member of senior exec team in governance group	Identify leaders and business sponsors of the transformation	Identify members of the transformation management team	The program manager & PMO. Project Mgrs. (when appropriate)	Representatives of the IT, HR and facility management teams	Define steering group for oversight & decision making
5.11 100 G	5.12 100 G	5.13 100 G	5.14 100 G	= 100 G	Status Green

Framework (5.2)

Objectives	Governance	Accountabilities	Risks and Issues	Meetings	
Define the objectives of the governance framework	Define the policies for governance of the governance team	Define roles and accountabilities for the governance team	Define the escalation process for issues, risks & security issues	Define the frequency of meetings, agendas and reporting	Create governance framework process for decision making
5.21 100 G	5.22 100 G	5.23 100 G	5.24 100 G	5.25 100 G	Status Green

PMO Govern (5.3)

PMO Charter	Data Reporting	Responsibilities	Decision Making	Outcomes	
Define the charter & guiding principles for the trans PMO	Determine the data and reporting needs for transformation	Create clear roles & responsibilities & publish a RACI	Determine the process for decision making & escalation	A Trans PMO focuses on a 360° view & program outcomes	Manage governance & progress at, program levels
5.31 100 G	5.32 100 G	5.33 100 G	5.34 100 G	5.35 100 G	Status Green

Program Plan (5.4)

Program Goals	Program Basics	Deliverables	Stakeholders	Program Metrics	
Review business case for the program and its objectives	Review scope, cost, and schedule, risks, the milestones	Review key program deliverables and timeline	Review stakeholders who need to be involved in program	Review program metrics on program performance	Review of program plans (progress, risks, schedule, budget)
5.41 100 G	5.42 100 G	5.43 100 G	5.44 100 G	5.45 100 G	Status Green

Change & Comms (5.5)

Change Vision	Resources	Assessment	Change Plans	Feedback	
Review the vision for change and the reasons for it	Ensure resources with change specialist skills & experience	Review ASIS and CIA assessment for defined TOBE change	Review change plan with appropriate comms and training	Review feedback on acceptance of change and change plan	OCM & comms are proactively actioned & reported
5.51 100 G	5.52 100 G	5.53 100 G	5.54 100 G	5.55 100 G	Status Green

Status Labels | Workstream No. | % complete | One red, then status red, One orange, then status orange, All green = Complete

I CANNOT SAY WHETHER THINGS WILL GET BETTER IF WE CHANGE; WHAT I CAN SAY IS THEY MUST CHANGE IF THEY ARE TO GET BETTER.

Georg Wilhelm Friedrich Hegel

The Master Plan

The one-page planning master program management plan is a document that outlines the process for managing the whole program. A comprehensive plan defines the key success areas of the program that capture the scope, objectives, and deliverables of the program, as well as the resources, budget, and timeline required to complete the program. The plan also outlines the roles and responsibilities of the program team, as well as the process for managing risks, issues, and stakeholders.

The purpose of the master plan is to provide a clear, concise, and consistent approach and the overall status of the program. It helps to ensure that the program stays on track, stays within budget, and delivers the desired results. The master one-page plan provides an important tool for communication, coordination, accountability and control which is essential for the successful delivery of a program.

Effective project resource management requires strong leadership, effective communication, and good organisation skills. It also requires the ability to plan and forecast resource needs, as well as the ability to manage and coordinate the use of resources across different teams and stakeholders.

This approach, along with supporting workstreams, helps to establish clear ownership and accountability for each key focus area of the program. This will help ensure that progress is made and that any challenges or issues are quickly addressed. This is a visible benefit of using the one-page planning process.

These workstreams are typically managed by an individual project manager and they are coordinated by the program manager, who is responsible for ensuring that all the necessary activities are completed and that the program is delivered successfully.

Starting a business transformation program can be a complex process and it is important to approach it carefully to ensure the best chances of success.

The Transformation Playbook

The Master Program Plan

Business Transformation - Master

Sponsor	Program Mgr.
O. Twist	B. Sykes
Completion Date	Overall Status
15th Feb 2024	Green

Goal: A successful business transformation with a seamless implementation & high user adoption where all stakeholders support and are engaged delivering all the desired business benefits, outcomes and improved customer experience (CX).

Key Areas	Workstreams Outcomes					Outcomes
Vision	**Strategy** — The current and future business strategy (goals and outcomes)	**Leadership** — Appoint a PM & leaders to provide program support	**Roadmap** — Develop a detailed roadmap of changes and deliverables	**Trans PMO** — Set up an agile PMO for the transformation and governance	**Resources** — Choose the right skilled people to plan & implement program	A clear strategy with a supporting roadmap with a PM, a PMO & right skilled people
1.0 J. Smith	1.1 100 G	1.2 100 G	1.3 100 G	1.4 100 G	1.5 100 G	Status Green
People	**Leadership** — Leaders & sponsors aligned on success criteria & strategy	**Stakeholders** — All stakeholders are identified for impact & program support	**Communications** — The change is made visible & way to grow engagement	**Change impact** — The impact level is measured & plan for readiness developed	**Training** — The competencies required are built into the training plan	All stakeholders support and embrace the vision and are engaged to support it
2.0 L. Baine	2.1 100 G	2.2 100 G	2.3 100 G	2.4 100 G	2.5 100 G	Status Green
Process	**CX Definition** — Define the desired CX in current marketplace & client expectations	**Process Analysis** — Target processes to transform to meet business & CX goals	**Process Testing** — Test the processes for performance before going live	**Application** — Implement the new processes with new documentation	**Impact Metrics** — Measure the impact of the new processes & refine where required	All processes been transformed to meet business & CX goals
3.0 K. West	3.1 100 G	3.2 100 G	3.3 100 G	3.4 100 G	3.5 100 G	Status Green
Technology	**Tech Team** — Create a cross functional team to assess ASIS tech	**ASIS State** — Assess existing tools & software to identify gaps & opportunities	**Tech Innovation** — Assess new tech for TOBE infrastructure to aid transformation	**Tech Application** — Implement new tech to support business strategy and goals	**Tech Metrics** — Measure success of new technologies for transformation	Implement new TOBE infrastructure to support strategy goals & improved CX
4.0 P. Giles	4.1 100 G	4.2 100 G	4.3 100 G	4.4 100 G	4.5 100 G	Status Green
Governance	**Steering Group** — Define steering group for oversight & decision making	**Framework** — Create governance framework process for decision making	**Trans PMO** — Manage progress at strategic, operation, and tactical levels	**Program Plan** — Review of program plans (progress, risks, schedule, budget)	**Change** — OCM & comms are proactively actioned & reported	Governance that aligns leadership & stakeholders with the change & program
5.0 B. Bass	5.1 100 G	5.2 100 G	5.3 100 G	5.4 100 G	5.5 100 G	Status Green

Status Labels | Workstream No. | % complete | Missed milestone, all status red, Going to miss milestone, status orange, All milestones met = Green

The master plan workstream activities

Vision	A clear strategy with a supporting roadmap with a PM, a PMO & right skilled people
People	All stakeholders support and embrace the vision and are engaged to support it
Process	All processes been transformed to meet business & CX goals
Technology	Implement new TOBE infrastructure to support strategy goals & improved CX
Governance	Governance that aligns leadership & stakeholders with the change & program
Transformation outcome	A successful business transformation with a seamless implementation & high user adoption where all stakeholders support and are engaged delivering all the desired business benefits, outcomes and improved customer experience (CX).

The master plan questions

Transformation goal	What is the goal of the transformation? What problem are you trying to solve, or what opportunity are you trying to seize?
Impacted stakeholders	Who will be impacted by the transformation, and who needs to be involved in the planning and execution?
Required resources	What resources (financial, human, technological) will be required to successfully complete the transformation?
Transformation timeline	What is the timeline for the transformation? What are the key milestones and deliverables?
Success measures	How will you measure the success of the transformation? What metrics will you use?
Risks and challenges	What risks and challenges do you anticipate, and how will you mitigate them?
Communications	How will you communicate and engage with stakeholders throughout the transformation process?

The master plan process

Program scope	Define the scope of the transformation program. Identify the specific areas of the business that you want to change and the goals you want to achieve.
Program sponsor	Find someone at the executive level who can provide leadership and support for the transformation program.
Assemble a team	Bring together a diverse group of people from across the organization to lead the transformation effort.
Roadmap	Create a plan that outlines the steps you will take to achieve your goals, including timelines and resources needed.
Communicate the vision	Clearly communicate the vision for the transformation to all stakeholders, including employees, customers, and partners.
Plan implementation	Execute the transformation plan, making any necessary adjustments along the way.
Measure progress	Regularly track progress and make adjustments as needed to ensure the transformation is on track.

The master plan outline

Vision & objectives	Define the vision and objectives for the business transformation. This includes identifying the problems or challenges that the transformation is intended to address, as well as the desired outcomes and benefits.
Business analysis	Conduct a thorough analysis of the current state of the business. This may include reviewing financial and operational performance, conducting customer and employee surveys, and assessing the firms' capabilities and resources.
Transformation plan	Develop a plan for the transformation, including a roadmap of specific initiatives and projects that will be undertaken. This should involve the identification of key stakeholders and the development of clear roles and responsibilities.
Communications	Communicate the transformation plan to employees and other stakeholders, and engage them in the process. This may involve training and development programs, as well as the creation of cross-functional teams to work on projects.
Implementation	Implement the transformation plan, including any necessary changes to systems, processes, and organizational structures. This may also involve the introduction of new technologies or the adoption of new business models.
Monitor & review progress	Monitor and review progress, and make any necessary adjustments to the transformation plan as the program progresses. Establish clear metrics and targets for tracking progress, as well as regular reporting to stakeholders.
Celebrate success	Celebrate success and recognise staff and other stakeholders who have contributed to the transformation.

The master plan deliverables

Overview	The goal of a business transformation plan is to provide a clear and comprehensive roadmap for making significant changes to the business to achieve its goals. It is is a roadmap for making significant changes to a business to achieve specific goals. The program deliverables of such a plan can vary depending on the specific nature of the transformation being undertaken and the business goals.
Vision and goals	A clear and detailed statement of the business's vision and goals, including the desired outcomes of the transformation.
Comprehensive analysis	A comprehensive analysis of the current state of the business, including its strengths and weaknesses, opportunities and threats, and the key drivers of its success or failure
A set of actionable recommendations	A set of specific and actionable recommendations for how to transform the business, including changes to its processes, systems, and organizational structure.
Timeline	A timeline for implementing the recommended changes, along with milestones & benchmarks for measuring progress.
Budget & resource plan	A budget and resource plan for executing the transformation, including estimates of the costs and the program benefits.
Risk management plan	A risk management plan, identifying the potential risks and challenges associated with the transformation, and outlining strategies for mitigating or avoiding them.
Communication & engagement plan	A communication and engagement plan, outlining how the business will engage and communicate with stakeholders throughout the transformation process.

The master plan best practices

Scope and objectives	Define the scope and objectives of the transformation program. Clearly articulate what you hope to achieve and the specific areas of the business that will be impacted.
Diverse team of stakeholders	Assemble a diverse team of stakeholders to help lead the transformation effort. This should include key leaders from across the organization, as well as representatives from different departments and levels.
ASIS assessment	Conduct a thorough assessment of the current state of the business, including its strengths, weaknesses, opportunities, and threats. This will help you identify areas for improvement and prioritize your efforts.
Transformation roadmap	Develop a roadmap for the transformation program, including a timeline, budget, and key milestones. Be sure to also identify any potential risks and plan for how to mitigate them.
Communication	Communicate the goals and progress of the transformation program to all employees, and seek their input and feedback throughout the process.
Ongoing measures	Continuously measure the success of the transformation program, and be willing to adjust your approach as needed based on the results you see.

The master plan risks

Cost risk	Business transformation programs can be costly, and there is always the risk that the costs will exceed the budget or that the benefits of the program will not justify the costs.
Scope creep	It can be difficult to maintain focus on the original goals of the program, and the scope may begin to expand beyond what was originally planned.
Insufficient planning	Failing to properly plan for the transformation can lead to a lack of clear goals and objectives, which can make it difficult to measure the success of the program.
Implementation risk	There is a risk that the program will not be implemented as planned, which can result in delays, cost overruns, or failure to achieve the desired outcomes.
Change management risk	Business transformation often involves significant changes to processes, systems, and organizational structures. People within the organization may resist changes to the way they work, which can make it difficult to implement new processes and systems.
Risk of failure	There is always the risk that a business transformation program will fail or not achieve the desired outcomes.
Individual dependencies	If key individuals leading the transformation leave the organization, it can disrupt the progress of the program.
Leadership support	If leadership does not fully support the transformation program, it can be difficult to get the necessary resources and buy-in from other stakeholders.

The master plan lessons learned

Plan for change management	Business transformation often involves significant changes to processes, systems, and even culture. It's important to have a plan in place to manage these changes and help ensure that they are smoothly and successfully implemented.
Key stakeholders	Involve key stakeholders from the outset, make sure that key stakeholders are involved in the planning and execution of the program. This will help ensure that their needs and concerns are taken into account, and that they are committed to the success of the program.
Proper planning	A key lesson learned is that proper planning is crucial. It is important to thoroughly plan a business transformation program, including identifying the goals, scope, budget, and resources required.
Communications	Communication is key, It is important to communicate the goals and progress of the program to all stakeholders, including employees, customers, and shareholders.
Budget control	Keep an eye on the budget as It is important to carefully monitor the budget and costs of a business transformation program to ensure that it stays on track and within budget.
Stay flexible	Business transformation programs can be complex and unpredictable, so it is important to be flexible and able to adapt to changing circumstances.
Challenges & setbacks	Be prepared for challenges and setbacks, transformation programs can be complex and challenging, and it's important to be prepared for setbacks and challenges along the way. It's important to have contingency plans in place, and to be flexible and adaptable in the face of changing circumstances.

THE ONLY PERSON YOU ARE DESTINED TO BECOME IS THE PERSON YOU DECIDE TO BE.

Ralph Waldo Emerson

1.0 Vision

An organisation that wants to change will have a vision for how their enhanced firm will appear. A vision is an image of how an organisation will appear in the future.

The vision presents the big picture and plainly explains what your company will look like in a few years. This makes the proper course of action clear so that everyone can proceed. Your plan is based on a vision statement. What we will become is addressed in the company's vision statement.

An excellent vision statement supports every aspect of a company's strategic orientation, making it beneficial to take the time to create the ideal company vision statement. If done correctly, it will be memorable, interesting, instructive, and motivating.

A business transformation vision is a long-term plan for achieving significant change in a company, it will include some of the following key aspects:

- A clear and compelling statement on the desired future state of the organisation.
- A roadmap for how to get there, including specific goals and objectives, and the strategies and tactics that will be used to achieve them.
- A clear understanding of the current state of the organisation and the challenges and opportunities it faces.
- A plan to engage and align stakeholders, including staff, customers, and other key groups, around the vision.
- A focus on continuous improvement, including the development of new skills, processes, and technologies that will enable the organisation to adapt to changing markets & customer needs.
- A plan to measure progress and success, including the development of key performance indicators (KPIs) to track progress towards vision.

1.0 Vision Plan Linkages

The Transformation Playbook

1.0 Vision Workstream Plan

Business Transformation: 1.0 Vision

Sponsor: O. Twist	**Program Mgr.:** B. Sykes
Completion: 15th Feb 2024	**Overall Status:** Green

Goal: A clear strategy with a supporting roadmap with a PM, an agile PMO & right skilled people

Workstreams / Workstreams Activities / Outcomes

Strategy (1.1)

ID	Activity	Description	Status
1.11	Current Strategy	Review the current and business strategy (goals and outcomes)	100 G
1.12	Vision & goals	Determine vision, goals, outcomes, tech, & processes for plan	100 G
1.13	Roadmap	Develop roadmap for program from the ASIS to TOBE state	100 G
1.14	Deliverables	Define the proposed deliverables of the transformation	100 G
1.15	Metrics	Identify metrics on how success will be measured	100 G

Outcome: The current and future business strategy (goals and outcomes) — Status: Green

Leadership (1.2)

ID	Activity	Description	Status
1.21	Program Mgr.	Appoint program manager for the transformation	100 G
1.22	Sponsor	Appoint executive sponsor for the program	100 G
1.23	Governance	Create governance group of key leaders for the program	100 G
1.24	Stakeholders	Identify impacted stakeholders by the program	100 G
1.25	PMO Leader	Appoint PMO leader to lead & manager the transformation status	100 G

Outcome: Appoint a PM & leaders to provide program support — Status: Green

Roadmap (1.3)

ID	Activity	Description	Status
1.31	ASIS Analysis	Review ASIS systems & processes for improvements	100 G
1.32	TOBE Design	Identify gaps & create desired outcome for transformation	100 G
1.33	Strategy Linkage	Review proposed changes to strategic goals and ROI	100 G
1.34	Goals	Set clear, realistic, measurable goals for transformation	100 G
1.35	Agile Approach	Adopt an agile phased approach including OCM throughout	100 G

Outcome: Develop a detailed roadmap of changes and deliverables — Status: Green

Agile PMO (1.4)

ID	Activity	Description	Status
1.41	PMO Charter	Create PMO charter that focuses on business value	100 G
1.42	PMO Leader	An agile PMO leader aligned to execution quality & transparency	100 G
1.43	Lean Portfolio	Program priorities aligned to value-add work streams & goals	100 G
1.44	Enterprise Focus	Delivery uses DevOps to coordinate work across streams	100 G
1.45	Agile Delivery	Agile project delivery used that begins with a customer focus	100 G

Outcome: Set up an agile PMO for the transformation and governance — Status: Green

Resources (1.5)

ID	Activity	Description	Status
1.51	Planning	Determine resource needs: type, skills for the program	100 G
1.52	Estimation	How much time will each resource need for program delivery	100 G
1.53	Acquisition	Obtain resources (internally / externally) with right skills	100 G
1.54	Agile Teams	Create agile cross functional teams that are customer focused	100 G
1.55	Evaluation	Monitor & evaluate resources to meet program needs	100 G

Outcome: Choose the right skilled people to plan & implement program — Status: Green

Status Labels: Workstream No. | % complete | Missed milestone, all status red, Going to miss milestone, status orange, All milestones met = Green

33

1.1 Strategy

The ideal way to begin a business transformation journey is to first create a vision that prioritises the demands of your consumers while also taking into account those of your staff, shareholders, and other stakeholders.

A business transformation strategy is a thorough plan for implementing digital technologies to enhance the efficiency of your company's operations and the quality of the services and products you offer to customers.

A wide business strategy is business transformation. A key building block is creating a strategy for short- and long-term digital transformation that is driven by business results rather than technology. In order to achieve critical corporate goals, it is crucial to develop a business transformation plan that is effective, quantifiable, and coordinated.

The ideal way to begin a business transformation journey is to first create a vision that prioritises the demands of your consumers while also taking into account those of your staff, shareholders, and other stakeholders.

A business transformation strategy is a thorough plan for implementing digital technologies to enhance the efficiency of your company's operations and the quality of the services and products you offer to customers.

A wide business strategy is business transformation. The key building block is creating a strategy for short- and long-term digital transformation that is driven by business results rather than technology. In order to achieve critical corporate goals, it is crucial to develop a business transformation plan that is effective, quantifiable, and coordinated.

Prepare for a change in culture, since people—not technology—are what drives business and digital transformation. Without a cohesive team, your digital strategy will fail before it ever leaves the dock. Finding the initial "proof-of-concept" project is essential since business transformation is a journey rather than an event. It will lay the groundwork for subsequent efforts and aid in gaining support from teams and leaders.

1.1 Strategy workstream activities

Current strategy	Review the current and business strategy (goals and outcomes)
Vision and goals	Determine vision, goals, outcomes. tech, & processes for plan
Roadmap	Develop roadmap for program from the ASIS to TOBE state
Deliverables	Define the proposed deliverables of the transformation
Metrics	Identify metrics on how success will be measured
Strategy outcome	The current and future business strategy (goals and outcomes)

1.1 Strategy questions

Transformation	What does business transformation entail?
Industry trends	What are the industry's business imperatives & trends?
Business opportunities	What opportunities will the digital shift bring?
Business clarity	Do the leaders understand the company's line of business?
Best decisions	What choices must the firm need to make for success?
Business priorities	What are the firm's business priorities and what is currently most important?
Key activities	What are the main things the firm can do to make the biggest difference & provide the best chance of success?
Barriers	What potential obstacles could impact the transformation?
Culture	What culture is required for a business transformation?
Starting point	With regard to transformation, where should the firm begin?

1.1 Strategy process

Vision and goals	Review and understand company vision and goals.
ASIS state	A company has to have a clear understanding of the true scope of the difficulties it faces before embarking on a business transformation initiative to address them.
Opportunities	Conduct an in-depth analysis of your current business model and identify business areas in need of change.
Executive buy-in	Gaining leadership support for transformation increases the likelihood that they will promote its importance to the firm.
Staff buy-in	An effective comms plan is key to staff understanding of what is happening in the firm before and after.
Cross-functional team	Build cross functional teams of staff & SMEs to collaborate and focus on transforming business process and customer experience with the use of new innovative technologies.
Agile program approach	Use an agile programme approach to transformation with a well-optimized plan to keep the business goals in mind.
Change management	Create an organisational change management plan. During corporate change, it is crucial to establish specific goals and let the staff know what they are. Changes within the firm come with business transformation and competent change management is essential for a successful outcome.
Monitor success	Develop KPIs and measure the success and progress of the transformational strategy.

1.1 Strategy plan components

General note on strategy	A business transformation strategy is not a one-time process, but rather an ongoing effort to continuously improve and adapt to the business changing needs and its customers.
The need for change	This could be due to a variety of factors such as changes in market conditions, new technology, or declining performance.
Transformation goals	Define the goals of the transformation. What do you hope to achieve through the transformation? Make goals SMART.
Business ASIS state	Analyse the current state of the business. This includes understanding the current processes, systems, and organizational structure.
Transformation roadmap	Develop a roadmap for the transformation. This should include specific action steps, timelines, and resources needed to achieve the desired goals.
implementation	Implement the transformation. This could involve making changes to processes, systems, and organizational structure. It may also involve training and upskilling employees.
Monitor & adjust	Keep track of progress and make adjustments as needed to ensure the transformation is successful.
Stakeholder communications	Keep all relevant parties informed about the transformation, including employees, customers, and shareholders.

1.1 Strategy best practices

Holistic approach	Review customer experience, operational processes and the business model from an enterprise perspective.
Key focus areas	Review goals, performance, KPIs, technology that supports the business systems, core processes, staff experience and skills, firm structure, governance and partnerships.
Client centred	The customer experience should come first. Determine customer's current perception and problems. Create customer profiles, pinpoint target market sand create a client journey map to reach customer experience goals.
Map current situation	Conduct an audit and map your present situation.
Seamless integration	Create a whole omnichannel of technologies that sync data, share information, and connect effortlessly.
Tech innovation	Make use of cutting-edge technologies: AI, cloud, IoT
Right staff, right skills	Employ the best staff to deliver a better customer experience.
Governance	A strong governance structure defines duties and creates procedures for updating leadership.

1.1 Strategy risks

Legacy systems	Obsolete, insecure, slow and inflexible technologies are among the top bottlenecks in business transformation.
Underestimating change	Many firms underestimates the challenges of implementing change especially within a culture that resists change and hinders growth. Any transformation effort's success or failure will depend on its strategy, communication, and engagement with the individuals it will most likely affect.
Technology focus	Successful corporate transformations go beyond simply installing new technologies to completely reimagine the employee or customer experience.
Budgeting	Budgeting and budget overruns can be a major issue when a business fails to see business transformation as a strategic investment and attempt to fund it as business as usual.
Silo thinking	Silos within organisations hinder business transformation as they can be a barrier in every stage of transformation.
Digital skills gap	Many firms attempting a transformation program find they lack digital skills (analytics, cloud, cybersecurity, enterprise architecture) and often have to see third party partner support.
Cybersecurity risks	Digitalisation has pushed security to the employees front-end and can increase a firm's vulnerability to increased cybersecurity risks without due diligence.
Executive buy in	It is not only a critical success factor to have leadership buy-in but also having a governance model outlines roles and establishes processes for keeping leadership informed.

1.1 Strategy lessons learned

Define the problem	Clearly define the business problem or opportunity that the transformation is intended to address. This will help ensure that the transformation efforts are focused and aligned with the overall business objectives.
Engage stakeholders from the start	Engage stakeholders early and often as It is important to involve key stakeholders in the strategy development process so that they feel invested in the transformation and can provide valuable insights and input.
A bigger view of the potential impact	Consider the potential impact on all areas of the business. Business transformation often involves changes to processes, systems, and organizational structures, so it is important to consider how these changes will affect different parts of the business.
Risk management	Develop a plan to manage and mitigate risks. Transformation can be risky, so it is important to identify potential risks and develop a plan to manage and mitigate them.
Communicate the strategy	Communicate the strategy and plan effectively. Clearly communicating the strategy and plan to all stakeholders will help ensure that everyone is aligned and working towards the same goals.
Be flexible	Be prepared to adapt and course correct as needed. Business transformation is an iterative process, and it is important to be flexible and adaptable in order to achieve the desired outcomes.

1.2 Leadership

Every business transformation necessitates a change in people, processes, and technology. Humans are reluctant to change by their nature. Significant organisational changes at people and process levels are required for digital transformation. When it comes to the staff, you need to give them the proper training and make them change-resistant. Additionally, organisational procedures need to be revised and reoriented toward corporate objectives.

Transformational leaders pay attention to the wants and concerns of their team members so they can help them appropriately. They work under the assumption that different people are motivated for different reasons. As a result, they can modify their management techniques to suit the needs of varied team members.

Business change agents and transformational leaders may spot emerging and changing technological trends and then assist their firms in embracing those changes. Transformational leaders are adept at inspiring and motivating their teams to act in ways that result in substantive change. A successful staff that is empowered to innovate and contribute to an organization's future success is the outcome.

Transformational leaders frequently question presumptions, take chances, and seek out the opinions and ideas of their teams. Instead of fostering a climate where it is unsafe to hold talks, be innovative, or speak different opinions, they do not fear failure. Employees are given more freedom to inquire, exercise more autonomy, and eventually choose more efficient ways to carry out their duties as a result.

1.2 Leadership workstream activities

Program manager	Appoint program manager for the transformation
Program sponsor	Appoint executive sponsor for the program
Governance group	Create governance group of key leaders for the program
Stakeholders	Identify impacted stakeholders by the program
PMO leader	Appoint PMO leader to lead & manager the transformation status
Leadership outcome	Appoint a PM & leaders to provide program support

1.2 Leadership questions

Program manager	**What is the role of a program manager?**
	A program manager ensures that all necessary steps have been taken to help the organisation achieve its goals, a program manager in for a business transformation initiative must be able to implement a thorough strategy for technology implementations with a strong response and communication system within the organisation. The transformation program manager is in charge of programs that result in significant changes for an organisation and are expected to produce business results within a predetermined range of constrained timeframes
Program sponsor	**What is the role of a program sponsor?**
	Program sponsors are often business executives who play a significant role in promoting, advocating for, and influencing program work or senior management members with a reasonable amount of influence and power. They are in charge of managing the program are responsible for ensuring that the promised benefits materialise over time.
Program governance	**What is the role of a program governance?**
	Enterprise-level platforms being implemented is a key goal of governance. Without solid leadership and governance, it can be very challenging to create an integrated perspective of operations or a single view of consumers. Governance for transformation (roadmaps, approach, change leadership structure, cross-functional decision rights, the organisational network required for the transformation, change relationships, roles and responsibilities, and the capabilities required.

1.2 Leadership questions

Stakeholders

What is the role of stakeholders in a program?

The main responsibility of a stakeholder is to aid an organisation in achieving its strategic goals by adding their expertise and viewpoint to a transformation programme.

Stakeholders can offer the resources and supplies needed. Since they have the greatest potential to affect the program's success, stakeholders must have a larger role in change efforts. Stakeholders need to publicly show their support for the change and accept it quickly. A business transformation initiative cannot be successful without their assistance.

PMO leader

What is the role of a Transformation PMO leader?

Transformation PMOs can ensure that a transformation strategy is in line with the overall strategy of the firm. Organizations can manage numerous programs and projects toward a single shared objective by using a TPMO.

A TPMO can assist in putting a strategy into action by gaining support from all important stakeholders which is one of the most important aspects of a successful business transformation. Stakeholders must understand the significance of the change, its potential advantages for the firm and what is it in it for them. Teams are more likely to desire to invest in business transformation initiatives by personalising the benefits of the change.

1.2 Leadership process

Define scope & goals	Clearly define what you want to achieve and why it is necessary.
Assemble a team	Bring together a diverse group of people who can help drive the change and ensure that all necessary functions and perspectives are represented.
Develop a roadmap	Create a plan for how the transformation will be implemented, including timelines, budgets, and key milestones.
Communicate the vision	Clearly communicate the vision for the transformation to stakeholders, including employees, customers, and shareholders.
Empower the team	Provide your team with the resources and support they need to succeed, and empower them to drive the change.
Monitor progress	Regularly assess progress against the roadmap and make adjustments as needed to ensure that the transformation stays on track.
Celebrate success	Recognize and celebrate the achievements of your team along the way.

1.2 Leadership best practices

Leaders with a clear vision for the firm	It is crucial to appoint leaders to oversee and support the business transformation initiative. Leader will need a vision for the business and a clear strategy to guide the firm in the creation of an in-depth business transformation roadmap. Employees should be motivated by transformational leaders who put a strong emphasis on their mission, values, and vision. Leaders can assist staff in realising that the work they do is important & beneficial to the business.
Experienced & skilled program manager	To assume overall responsibility for guaranteeing the change is carried out without difficulty, on schedule, and within budget, a programme manager is selected. To accomplish a successful change, the program manager will need the appropriate experience and skills.
Stakeholders	It is important that all stakeholders impacted by the change are identified, engaged and regularly communicated to.
PMO	A PMO leader needs to be flexible, agile and focus on successful outcomes rather than traditional bureaucracy.
Change management	It is a critical success factor that an organisational change management plan is developed at the start of a program.
Staff development	The ability for workers to benefit from opportunities to advance their abilities should be fostered by leaders. For a team under the direction of a transformative leader, learning and training should never end. Make coaching and mentorship a priority with plans to coach and mentor staff.

1.2 Leadership risks

Resistance to change	The main cause of this resistance to change impact, or at least what aggravates it, is poor communication. A clear vision & openness with staff will help to win their support.
Focus & concentration	A lack of concentration on important tasks might result from lack of motivation among team members, which is how transformational leadership works. Transformative leaders should establish clear expectations for each member of their team in order to solve the issue of lack of concentration. Issues may be prevented with focus by integrating task management into the culture.
No appetite for risk	Leaders that are transformational take calculated risks that almost always have a favourable consequence. It's crucial they trust their instincts and the intelligence their teams collects. When they have taken the time to investigate, assess, and inform their decisions with advice from their peers and staff, it is simpler to trust their instinct.
Willingness to listen	Transformational leaders are aware that progress comes from the desire to be receptive to ideas from all tiers of their business and that success is a team effort. Transformational leaders design deliberate processes for hearing from and including their team.
Burnout avoidance	Effective transformational leaders encourage their staff to take advantage of paid time off and other benefits. They also devise strategies for routinely celebrating the accomplishments of their workforce.

1.2 Leadership lessons learned

Communicate the vision	Clearly communicate the vision and goals of the program: It's important to clearly communicate the vision and goals of the transformation program to all stakeholders, including employees, customers, and shareholders. This helps to ensure that everyone is on the same page and working towards a common goal.
Involve staff in the planning	Involving employees in the planning process can help to build buy-in and ownership for the program. This can be done through focus groups, surveys, and employee workshops.
Be adaptable	Business transformation programs often involve making changes to processes, systems, and organizational structures. It's important to be adaptable and flexible, and to be willing to make course corrections as needed.
A culture of continuous improvement	Foster a culture of continuous improvement. A culture of continuous improvement can help to ensure that the business transformation program is successful and sustainable. Encourage employees to identify areas for improvement and to propose solutions.
Stay focused on the long-term	It's important to stay focused on the long-term goals of the transformation program, even when faced with short-term challenges or setbacks. This requires strong leadership and the ability to maintain a long-term perspective.

1.3 Roadmap

Making substantial changes to the way a corporation or organisation operates is referred to as "business transformation."

A business transformation roadmap is a plan that outlines the steps and resources needed to achieve a desired change or improvement in an organization. Personnel, procedures, and technology are all included in this. Organizations that undergo these changes are better able to compete, become more efficient, or completely change their strategic direction.

The multi-step process of digitization necessitates careful planning and a sound strategy. Consequently, a company transformation plan lays out the activities it can take to fulfil its digitalization objectives. A roadmap for digital transformation is a strategy that takes your business from the ASIS state (using the processes and technology infrastructure that is currently used) to the TOBE state (using newly transformed business processes supported by new digital technologies).

A roadmap begins with the identification of your objectives and the outcomes you hope to attain. The second step is to assess the current situation, which entails looking at your organization's internal and external environments.

The investigation will include identifying which organisational processes are not technology-powered, where the gap is, and how digitalization may fill it.

A firm can move on to develop tactics to get there after they are aware of its strategic objectives, existing state, and goals. In order to make transformation a reality and a success, the implementation plans may involve several elements, such as updating their infrastructure and key business processes, making investments in cutting-edge and developing technologies, and recruiting the appropriate personnel.

Once the commitment of the leadership has been established and a transformation budget is available, the implementation plan should be broken down into manageable, brief phases.

To get a rapid win within the organisation, starting with a pilot project is always recommended practice

1.3 Roadmap workstream activities

ASIS analysis	Review ASIS systems & processes. Identify improvements
TOBE design	Identify gaps & create desired outcome for transformation
Strategy linkage	Review proposed changes to strategic goals and ROI
Goals and objectives	Set clear, realistic, measurable goals for transformation
Agile and change	Adopt an agile phased approach including OCM throughout.
Roadmap outcome	Develop a detailed roadmap of changes and deliverables

1.3 Roadmap questions

Leadership knowledge	**What is the leadership knowledge of digitisation?**
	The leadership have a thorough understanding of the implications of digital and technology to offer insightful direction for a business transformation, or do they need to employ a partner to fill in the knowledge & skills gaps?
The Transformation	**Is the planned business transformation bold enough?**
	The planned business transformation is bold with a long-term view to transform the business and its customer value.
Company goals	**Is there a clear vision?**
	There a clear vision and supporting goals for the roadmap.
The ASIS state	**Has the processes & infrastructure been analysed?**
	The current processes and infrastructure have been analysed for issues, gaps and opportunities.

1.3 Roadmap questions

Implementation Plans	**Have all key stakeholders engaged in planning?**
	All impacted leaders & staff been involved in the creation of the implementation plans derived from the roadmap.
Program Funding	**Is there a separate Transformation budget?**
	There is separate funding that has been made available to fund the transformation and beyond business as usual?
Leadership commitment	**Is the leadership committed to the transformation?**
	The leaders been engaged on the development of the roadmap and they are committed to is successful completion.
Metrics	**Have metrics been agreed, aligned and developed?**
	Metrics have been agreed, aligned and developed to measure the success of the transformation during the implementation of the roadmap.
Right people, right skills	**Are the right people with the right skills in place?**
	This is a repetitive question but many firms fail to recognise the importance of having the right specialist skills for success of a business transformation/

1.3 Roadmap process

Business objectives	Start by understanding the business objectives that the transformation program is trying to achieve. This will help you align your efforts with the overall goals of the organization.
Stakeholder inputs	Engage with stakeholders across the organization to gather input on the challenges and opportunities that the transformation program should address. This could include staff, customers, and partners.
Business analysis	Analyse the current state of the business and identify areas for improvement. This could include reviewing financial data, customer feedback, and internal processes.
Program scope	Based on the input gathered from stakeholders and the business analysis, define the scope of the transformation program. This should include a clear description of the specific goals and objectives of the program.
Roadmap	Use the information gathered in the previous steps to create a roadmap that outlines the steps needed to achieve the objectives of the transformation program. The roadmap should include key milestones and a timeline for completion.
Communicate roadmap	Share the roadmap with relevant stakeholders to ensure that everyone is aligned on the goals and objectives of the transformation program. Make sure to communicate any updates or changes to the roadmap as needed.
Implement & monitor	Put the roadmap into action and track progress towards achieving the objectives of the transformation program. Regularly review and update the roadmap as needed to ensure that the program stays on track.

1.3 Roadmap plan components

General outline	This is just a general outline and each business transformation roadmap will be unique depending on the specific needs and goals of the organization.
The need for change	Identify the need for change. This could be due to internal or external factors such as changes in the market, new technologies, or shifts in customer needs.
Goals & objectives	Set goals and objectives. Clearly define what you hope to achieve through the transformation and how it aligns with your overall business strategy
ASIS assessment	Conduct a current state assessment. Understand the current state of your business, including processes, technologies, and organizational structure.
The TOBE state definition	Define the future state. Based on the goals and current state assessment, determine what the future state of the business should look like. This may include changes to processes, technologies, and/or organizational structure.
A plan to move from the ASIS to the TOBE	Create a detailed plan outlining the steps needed to move from the current state to the future state. This should include timelines, budgets, and resources required.
Implement the plan	Put the plan into action, making any necessary changes to processes, technologies, and the organizational structure.
Monitor and adjust	Continuously monitor the progress of the transformation and make adjustments as needed to ensure that the business is on track to achieve its goals.

1.3 Roadmap best practices

Clear goals	The transformation's goals and desired results should be properly stated. This will make it possible to track progress and ensure that the roadmap is in line with the organization's overarching objectives.
Realistic expectations	By being cautious of false assumptions, realistic expectations, goals, and milestones that build up a company's business transformation can be developed.
Stakeholders	Involve key stakeholders in the planning process. This can help ensure that the transformation takes into account the needs and perspectives of different departments and teams within the organization.
Roadmap phases	Break the transformation roadmap down into smaller, manageable phases and steps. This can help make the process more manageable and reduce the risk of setbacks.
Prioritize initiatives	Identify and prioritize key initiatives. This can help ensure that resources are focused on the most important initiatives and that progress is made on the most critical areas first.
Accountability	Establish clear ownership and accountability for each initiative. This can help ensure that progress is made and that any challenges or issues are quickly addressed. This is a visible benefit of using the one-page planning process.
Regula reviews	Regularly review and adjust the roadmap as needed. This can help ensure that the transformation stays on track and that any changes in the business are taken into account.

The Transformation Playbook

1.3 Roadmap risks

Stakeholder buy-in	Lack of buy-in from key stakeholders: If key stakeholders do not understand or support the roadmap, it may be difficult to get the resources and support needed to successfully execute the transformation.
Unrealistic timelines	If the timeline for the transformation is too aggressive, it may be difficult to achieve the desired outcomes within the allotted time frame.
Scope creep	If the scope of the transformation changes significantly over time, it can lead to delays and cost overruns.
Inadequate resources	Inadequate resources: A lack of sufficient resources, such as funding, personnel, or technology, can hinder progress and increase the risk of failure. Business transformation initiatives requires significant resources, including budget, experienced and skilled people, and time. It is important to allocate these resources appropriately to ensure that the transformation is successful.
Build in flexibility	If the scope of the transformation changes significantly over time, it can lead to delays and cost overruns.
Resistance to change	Some employees may resist the changes outlined in the roadmap, which can make it difficult to successfully implement the transformation.

1.3 Roadmap lessons learned

Clear goals	Having clear goals is not only a best practice but key lessons are often learned from not having them. Clearly define the goals and objectives: It is important to have a clear understanding of what the organization wants to achieve through the digital transformation. This will help to align the roadmap with the overall business strategy and ensure that the resources invested in the transformation are focused on delivering the desired results.
Stakeholder engagement	It is important to involve key stakeholders in the process of creating your roadmap. This will help ensure that their needs and concerns are taken into account, and will also help build buy-in and support for the program.
Detailed roadmap	A business transformation roadmap should be derailed and cover all aspects of the transformation, including technology, processes, people, and culture. This will help to ensure that all necessary changes are identified & addressed. Your roadmap should include a timeline that outlines the expected completion date for each project or initiative. This will help ensure that the program stays on track and achieves its aims.
Prioritize projects	In order to achieve your goals, you will need to identify and prioritize specific projects and initiatives. Consider using a tool like the Lean Business Model Canvas to help identify key areas of focus and prioritize projects based on their impact.
Build in flexibility	The digital landscape is constantly evolving, and it is important to be flexible and adaptable in order to stay ahead of the curve. It is important to regularly review and adjust the business transformation roadmap as needed to ensure that it remains relevant and effective.

1.4 Agile PMO

A traditional Project Management Office (PMO) is an organizational unit or group within a company that is responsible for establishing and maintaining standards for project management within the organization. The primary focus of a traditional PMO is to provide support for project managers and to ensure that projects are completed on time, within budget, and to the required quality standards.

An agile transformational PMO, on the other hand, is focused on driving change and transformation within an organization. It is often responsible for leading and coordinating large-scale change initiatives, such as the implementation of new business processes or the adoption of new technologies.

An agile transformational PMO may also provide support and guidance to project managers and teams, but its primary focus is on driving change and organizational improvement.

An agile transformational PMO that is responsible for the planning, execution, and governance of projects.

In an agile transformational PMO, the focus is on continuous improvement and the agile philosophy is embraced. This means that the PMO is flexible and responsive to change, and is able to adapt to the needs of the organization and its stakeholders.

Overall, a transformational agile PMO aims to provide a holistic approach to project management that promotes collaboration, transparency, and continuous improvement.

1.4 Agile PMO workstream activities

Agile PMO charter	Create PMO charter that focuses on business-driven value
PMO leader	An agile PMO leader aligned to execution quality & transparency
Lean portfolio mgt.	Program priorities aligned to value-add work streams & goals
Enterprise focus	Delivery uses DevOps to coordinate work across workstreams
Agile delivery	Agile project delivery used that begins with a customer focus
Agile PMO outcome	Set up an agile PMO for the transformation and governance

1.4 Agile PMO questions

PMO charter	**What is a PMO charter?**
	A PMO charter is a document that outlines the purpose, roles, responsibilities, and functions of a PMO within an organization. The charter is used to establish the PMO's authority, align the PMO's gaols with those of the firm, and define the PMO's relationship with other departments.
PMO leader	**What are the qualities of an agile PMO leader?**
	An agile transformational PMO leader is able to effectively guide and support a firm through a transition to an agile way of working with some key qualities such as: • An ability to be flexible and adapt to changing circumstances is essential in an agile environment. An agile transformational PMO leader should be able to quickly adjust plans and strategies as needed. • An agile transformational PMO leader should be able to effectively collaborate with their team members and stakeholders to ensure that everyone is aligned. • Strong communication skills are essential for an agile transformational PMO leader, as they will need to be able to clearly convey ideas and expectations to team members and stakeholders. • An agile transformational PMO leader should be able to identify and solve problems that arise during the agile transformation process. • An agile transformational PMO leader should be able to inspire and motivate team members to work towards the organization's goals, and should be able to effectively manage and delegate tasks as needed.

1.4 Agile PMO questions

Lean portfolio mgt.	**What is lean portfolio management?**
	Lean portfolio management is a set of principles and practices that focus on maximizing value and minimizing waste in the management of a firm's portfolio of work.
DevOps	**What is DevOps?**
	DevOps is a software engineering culture and practice that aims to unify software development (Dev) and software operation (Ops). The goal of DevOps is to shorten the systems development life cycle and provide continuous delivery with high software quality.
	DevOps emphasizes collaboration, communication, and integration between software developers and IT operations professionals. By promoting a culture of collaboration and automation, DevOps aims to increase an organization's ability to deliver applications and services at high velocity.
	With the use of agile software development methodologies, which focus on rapid iteration & the continuous delivery & testing of small software increments.
Agile project delivery	**What is Agile project delivery?**
	Agile project delivery is an approach to managing and completing projects that is characterized by flexibility and rapid adaptation to change. It is based on the Agile Manifesto, a set of values and principles that prioritize customer satisfaction, rapid delivery of high-quality products, and the ability to respond to change.

1.4 Agile PMO process

PMO purpose	Define the purpose and scope of the Agile PMO for the business transformation program. Determine the specific goals and objectives that the PMO will be responsible for and how it will support agile teams.
PMO resources	Identify the resources needed for the PMO. This may include personnel, tools, and budget.
Governance	Establish governance and decision-making processes aligned with business transformation governance. Determine how the PMO will be governed and how decisions will be made within the PMO.
Agile practices	Implement agile practices within the PMO that will aid the business transformation. This may include adopting agile methodologies such as Scrum or Kanban, implementing agile tools &techniques, and training PMO staff in agile principles.
PMO reporting	Establish communication and reporting processes to meet the needs of the business transformation program. Determine how the PMO will communicate with agile teams and stakeholders, and establish reporting processes to track progress and identify areas for improvement.
Ongoing improvements	Review and continuously improve the PMO. Regularly review the effectiveness of the PMO and make changes as needed to improve its performance and support for agile teams.

1.4 Agile PMO plan components

General note	Here is an example outline for an agile PMO as part of a business transformation strategy:
Purpose of the PMO	Define the purpose and scope of the PMO. Identify the specific areas where the PMO will provide value and support.
Steering committee	Establish a steering committee of senior leaders and representatives from each business unit to ensure that the PMO has the support and guidance it needs to be successful.
PMO operating model	Define the PMO's operating model to include the roles and responsibilities of the PMO team, and processes and tools.
PMO team	Build the PMO team. Identify and recruit individuals with the skills & expertise necessary to support agile project delivery.
PMO roadmap	Develop the PMO's roadmap: This roadmap should outline the key initiatives and priorities for the PMO over the next year, as well as the steps necessary to achieve them
Agile governance	Implement agile governance to support project delivery, including agile project management, agile estimation and planning, and agile reporting and metrics.
Agile training & coaching	Provide training and coaching to project teams and PMO staff so everyone is familiar with agile practices & can apply them.
Agile metrics & reporting	Set up systems to track and report on agile project delivery, including KPIs and other metrics.
Continuous improvement	Regularly review and assess the effectiveness of the PMO's processes and practices, and make changes as needed to ensure ongoing success.

1.4 Agile PMO best practices

PMO charter contents	It is a best practice that a PMO charter includes: • The PMO purpose and the goals it is expected to achieve. • The scope of the PMO, including the types of projects it will support and the methods it will use. • The roles and responsibilities of PMO staff and the authority they have to make decisions and take actions. • The relationships and interfaces between the PMO and other departments, stakeholders, and external partners. • The governance structure of the PMO, including the decision-making processes and reporting structures. • The resources that will be made available to the PMO, including staff, budget, and technology. • The performance metrics that will be used to measure the success of the PMO.
Lean portfolio management	Best practices for implementing lean portfolio management: • Clearly define the value that the portfolio is expected to deliver, and align all activities with this value proposition. • Use a prioritization process to identify the most valuable work and allocate resources accordingly. • Use metrics to measure the value delivered by the portfolio and track progress towards goals. • Use a continuous improvement process to identify and eliminate waste in the portfolio management process. • Foster collaboration and transparency across the organization to ensure that all stakeholders are aligned on the goals and priorities of the portfolio. • Use lean governance principles to make decisions quickly and efficiently, while minimizing bureaucracy. • Adopt agile delivery methods to enable rapid iteration and delivery of value.

1.4 Agile PMO best practices

DevOps	There are several best practices that are commonly followed in DevOps environments: • This involves regularly integrating code changes into a shared code repository, and automatically building and testing the code to ensure it is in a deployable state. • This includes automatically building, testing, and releasing code changes to production, with the ability to roll back changes if necessary. • Monitoring the performance of applications in production can help identify and resolve issues quickly. • Encouraging collaboration between development and operations teams can help improve communication and facilitate faster problem resolution. • Using version control systems can help track changes to code and manage multiple versions of software. • Implementing robust testing practices, including unit testing, integration testing, and acceptance testing, can help ensure the quality of software releases.
Agile project delivery	In an agile project, it is a best practice that teams follow a set of iterative and incremental development processes, often referred to as "sprints," to deliver functional increments of a product or service. The team works collaboratively with the customer to define and prioritize the features and requirements for the product, and then delivers those features in short, iterative cycles. The team also regularly reviews and adjusts its plans and priorities based on feedback from the customer and other stakeholders.

1.4 Agile PMO risks

Executive support	An agile transformation requires a culture shift and buy-in from leadership. Without the support of executives, it can be difficult to successfully implement an agile transformation.
No PMO charter	It is a risk if a PMO charter is not in place. It is an important document that helps to ensure that the PMO is aligned with the overall goals of the organization and that it is able to effectively support the delivery of projects. It is developed by the PMO team in collaboration with key stakeholders.
Resistance to change	One of the biggest risks of ay transformation is resistance to change from stakeholders who may be comfortable with the current processes and tools. It's important to communicate the transformation benefits and involve stakeholders in the planning process to increase buy-in and minimize resistance.
Cookie cutter agile	Agile is not a one-size-fits-all approach, and it's important to tailor the framework to the needs and goals of the organization. Failing to do so can lead to the adoption of practices that are not effective or sustainable.
Agile training	Another risk is inadequate training for staff on agile principles and practices. It's important to provide ongoing training and support to ensure that team members have the knowledge and skills needed to effectively implement agile.
Insufficient resources	Implementing an agile transformation can also require additional specialist resources and tools for planning and implementing change as well having a good understanding of agile practices. It's important to ensure that these resources are available and properly allocated.

1.4 Agile PMO lessons learned

Start small	Start small and focus on building momentum. It is important to start with a small, manageable set of projects and build momentum from there. This helps to demonstrate the value of the PMO and build buy-in from stakeholders.
Ongoing improvement	Foster a culture of continuous improvement. An Agile PMO should be focused on continuous improvement and should encourage teams to continuously reflect on their processes and identify ways to improve.
Flexible & adaptable	Agile methodologies are all about being flexible and adaptable to change. The PMO should embrace this mindset and be willing to pivot and change course as needed.
Focus on value delivery	The PMO should focus on delivering value to stakeholders and customers, rather than just following a rigid plan.
Stakeholder relationships	Build strong relationships with stakeholders. The PMO should work closely with stakeholders to understand their needs and priorities & ensure projects are aligned with business goals.
PMO has the right skills & resources	Make sure the PMO has the right skills and resources. It is important to ensure that the PMO has the necessary skills and resources to effectively support Agile projects. This may require training and hiring new staff with relevant experience.

1.5 Resources

Project resource management is the process of effectively organizing, utilizing, and directing the people, tools, and materials needed to complete a project. It involves identifying the resources that are required to complete the project, acquiring those resources, and then managing them effectively throughout the project.

Effective project resource management is crucial for ensuring that a project is completed on time, within budget, and to the required quality standards. It involves managing various types of resources, including human resources (such as project team members), material resources (such as equipment and supplies), and financial resources (such as budget and funding).

The goal of project resource management is to ensure that the right resources are available when and where they are needed, and that they are used efficiently and effectively.

This may involve creating a project resource plan, which outlines the specific resources that will be needed and how they will be used, and then monitoring and adjusting the plan as the project progresses.

Effective project resource management requires strong leadership, effective communication, and good organization skills. It also requires the ability to plan and forecast resource needs, as well as the ability to manage and coordinate the use of resources across different teams and stakeholders.

1.5 Resources workstream activities

Resource planning	Determine resource requirements, type, skills for the program
Resource estimation	How much time will each resource need for program delivery
Acquire resources	Obtain right resources (internally / externally) with right skills
Agile teams	Create agile cross functional teams that are customer focused
Resource evaluation	Continually monitor & evaluate resources to meet program needs
Resources outcome	Choose the right skilled people to plan & implement program

1.5 Resources questions

Resource types	What resources are required for the project?
Resource availability	How much of each resource is needed, and when will it be needed?
Resource acquisition	Who will be responsible for acquiring the resources?
Acquisition method	How will the resources be acquired?
Resource use	How will the resources be used most efficiently?
Resource management	How will the use of resources be monitored and controlled?
Resource changes	How will changes to the resource plan be managed?
Specialist training	How will the project team be trained on the use of any specialized resources?
Resource risks	How will any risks associated with acquiring or using resources be managed?

1.5 Resources process

Resource management	Resource management in a business transformation program is the process of identifying, acquiring, and organizing the human, financial, and technological resources needed to successfully implement the program.
Resource requirements	The first step in resource management is to identify the resources that are needed to successfully implement the transformation program. This might include human resources, such as employees or contractors, financial resources, such as budget or funding, and technological resources, such as software or hardware.
Acquire resources	Once you have identified the resources you need, you will need to acquire them. This might involve hiring new employees, securing funding, or purchasing technology.
Organize resources	Once you have acquired the resources you need, you will need to organize them in a way that allows you to effectively implement the transformation program. This might involve creating teams, assigning tasks, and setting up systems for tracking progress.
Monitor & adjust	As the transformation program progresses, you will need to continually monitor the resources you have available and make adjustments as needed. This might involve reallocating resources or acquiring additional resources to ensure that the program is successful.

1.5 Resources plan components

General note	The specific details of the resource management plan will depend on the nature of the business and the goals of the transformation strategy.
Scope and goals	Define the scope and goals of the transformation strategy.
Resources identification	Identify the resources needed to execute the strategy, including personnel, equipment, technology, and budget.
Resource allocation plan	Develop a plan to allocate and utilize these resources effectively, including any necessary training or development.
Resource metrics	Establish metrics for tracking and measuring the effectiveness of the resource management plan.
Resource reviews	Regularly review and adjust the plan as needed to ensure alignment with the overall business transformation strategy.

1.5 Resources best practices

Resource identification	Identify and document the resources required to complete the project. This includes human resources, equipment, materials, and financial resources.
Resource planning	Develop a plan to acquire the necessary resources. This may involve hiring staff, purchasing equipment, or negotiating contracts with vendors.
Resource monitoring	Monitor resource usage and track costs throughout the project. This helps to ensure that the project stays within budget and that resources are used efficiently.
Resource reviews	Regularly review and adjust the resource plan as needed. As a program progresses, the resource requirements may change. It is key to reassess and adjust the plan to ensure that the project has the resources it needs to be successful.
Resource comms	Communicate with team members about resource availability and allocation. Make sure that everyone understands how resources are being used and how they can access the resources they need to do their work.
Resource tools	Use PM software to help manage resources. There are many tools available that can help you track and manage resources, including project scheduling software, budget tracking software, and time tracking software.

1.5 Resources risks

Cost overruns	If resources are not managed properly, the cost of the transformation program may exceed the budget, leading to financial problems for the company.
Delays	Poor resource management can lead to delays in the completion of the transformation program, which can impact the timeline and goals of the project.
Quality issues	If resources are not properly managed, it can lead to a decrease in the quality of the work being done, which can have negative impacts on the company's reputation and bottom line.
Employee burnout	If employees are overworked or not given the resources, they need to complete their tasks, it can lead to burnout and a decrease in morale.
Stakeholder dissatisfaction	If stakeholders are not kept informed about the progress of the transformation program, or if the program does not meet their expectations, it can lead to dissatisfaction and potentially damage relationships with key stakeholders.

1.5 Resources risks

Cost overruns	If resources are not managed properly, the cost of the transformation program may exceed the budget, leading to financial problems for the company.
Delays	Poor resource management can lead to delays in the completion of the transformation program, which can impact the timeline and goals of the project.
Quality issues	If resources are not properly managed, it can lead to a decrease in the quality of the work being done, which can have negative impacts on the company's reputation and bottom line.
Employee burnout	If employees are overworked or not given the resources, they need to complete their tasks, it can lead to burnout and a decrease in morale.
Stakeholder dissatisfaction	If stakeholders are not kept informed about the progress of the transformation program, or if the program does not meet their expectations, it can lead to dissatisfaction and potentially damage relationships with key stakeholders.

1.5 Resources lessons learned

Misaligned goals	It's important to ensure that the goals of the project and the allocation of resources are aligned. If the goals of the project and the resources allocated do not align, it can lead to wasted resources and project failure.
Insufficient resources	It's important to accurately estimate the resources required for a transformation program and ensure that they are available when needed. This is a common cause of failure when firms fail to recognise the require specialist skills and experience for a business transformation not always available inside a company.
Unclear roles and responsibilities	Clearly defined roles and responsibilities can help ensure that resources are used effectively and efficiently.
Poor communications	Effective communication is key to successful resource management. Regular meetings and updates can help ensure that all team members are aware of resource availability and utilization for a transformation program.
Lack of flexibility	It's important to be flexible and adaptable in resource management, as changes to a project can often require adjustments to resource allocation. This is why an agile PMO is required for a successful transformation as they are flexible and focus on results not bureaucracy.

CHANGE IS THE ONLY CONSTANT IN LIFE.

Plato

2.0 People

Business transformation programs involve significant changes to the way a business operates, and these changes can have a significant impact on the people who work for the business. Therefore, it is important to consider the people aspect in a business transformation program to ensure that the changes are successful and sustainable.

Some of the key ways in which the people aspect is important in a business transformation program include:

- Ensuring that the necessary skills and knowledge are present within the organization to support the transformation. This may involve training and development programs to help employees adapt to the new way of working.

- It is common for people to resist change, particularly when it involves significant shifts in the way they work. Therefore, it is important to manage this resistance and to engage with employees to help them understand the rationale behind the transformation and how it will benefit them.

- Business transformations can be disruptive and challenging, and it is important to ensure that employees remain motivated and engaged throughout the process. This may involve providing support and resources to help employees adapt to the new way of working.

- A successful business transformation program should encourage a culture of continuous improvement.

2.0 People Plan Linkages

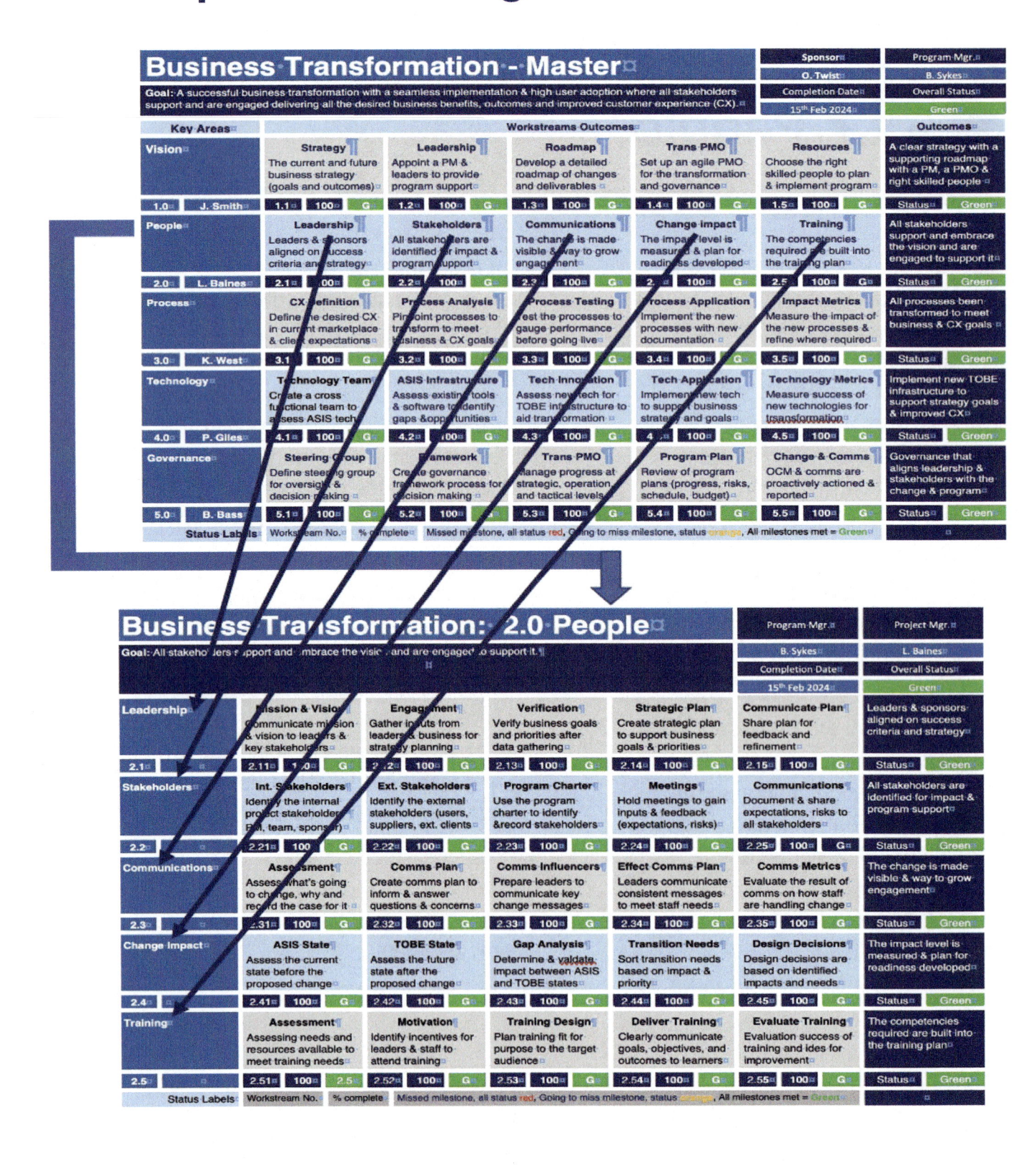

2.0 People Workstream Plan

Business Transformation: 2.0 People

Goal: All stakeholders support and embrace the vision and are engaged to support it.

	Program Mgr.	Project Mgr.
	B. Sykes	L. Baines
	Completion Date	Overall Status
	15th Feb 2024	Green

Leadership (2.1)

Mission	Engagement	Verification	Strategic Plan	Comms Plan	Leaders & sponsors aligned on success criteria and strategy
Communicate mission & vision to leaders & key stakeholders	Gather inputs from leaders & business for strategy plans	Verify business goals and priorities after data gathering	Create strategic plan to support business goals & priorities	Share plan for feedback and refinement	
2.11 / 100 / G	2.12 / 100 / G	2.13 / 100 / G	2.14 / 100 / G	2.15 / 100 / G	Status: Green

Stakeholders (2.2)

Stakeholders	Suppliers	Charter	Meetings	Comms	All stakeholders are identified for impact & program support
Identify the internal stakeholders (PM, team, sponsor)	Identify the ext. stakeholders: users, suppliers, clients	Use the program charter to identify & note stakeholders	Hold meetings to gain inputs & expectations, feedback & risks	Document & share expectations, risks to all stakeholders	
2.21 / 100 / G	2.22 / 100 / G	2.23 / 100 / G	2.24 / 100 / G	2.25 / 100 / G	Status: Green

Comms (2.3)

Assessment	Comms Plan	Influencers	Comms Plan	Comms Metrics	The change is made visible to grow engagement
Assess what's going to change, why and record the case for it	Create comms plan to inform & answer questions & concerns	Prepare leaders to communicate key change messages	Leaders convey consistent messages to meet staff needs	Evaluate the result of comms on how staff are handling change	
2.31 / 100 / G	2.32 / 100 / G	2.33 / 100 / G	2.34 / 100 / G	2.35 / 100 / G	Status: Green

Change Impact (2.4)

ASIS State	TOBE State	Gap Analysis	Transition	Decisions	The impact level is measured & plan for readiness developed
Assess the current state before the proposed change	Assess the future state after the proposed change	Determine & validate impact between ASIS and TOBE states	Sort transition needs based on impact & priority	Design decisions are based on identified impacts and needs	
2.41 / 100 / G	2.42 / 100 / G	2.43 / 100 / G	2.44 / 100 / G	2.45 / 100 / G	Status: Green

Training (2.5)

Assessment	Motivation	Training Design	Deliver Training	Evaluation	The competencies required are built into the training plan
Assessing needs and resources available to meet training needs	Identify incentives for leaders & staff to attend training	Plan training fit for purpose to the target audience	Clearly convey goals, objectives, and outcomes to learners	Evaluation success of training and ides for improvement	
2.51 / 100 / 2.5	2.52 / 100 / G	2.53 / 100 / G	2.54 / 100 / G	2.55 / 100 / G	Status: Green

Status Labels | Workstream No. | % complete | Missed milestone, all status red, Going to miss milestone, status orange, All milestones met = Green

2.1 Leadership

Business transformation is a process of fundamentally changing how a business operates in order to improve its performance and adapt to changes in its environment. Successful business transformation requires effective and inspiration leadership.

There are many qualities that are important for leaders in today's business environment. One key leadership quality is emotional intelligence which refers to the ability to understand and manage your own emotions, as well as the emotions of others. It is important for leaders to be able to build strong, positive relationships with their team members and stakeholders.

The business world is constantly changing, and leaders need to be able to adapt to new situations and challenges. This means being open to new ideas and approaches, and being able to pivot when necessary.

Leaders need to be able to think ahead and plan for the long-term success of their organizations. This means being able to identify opportunities, set goals, and create a vision for the future.

Effective communication is essential for leaders to be able to convey their ideas and plans to their team and stakeholders. This includes the ability to listen, speak, and write clearly and effectively. A leader must be able to clearly and effectively communicate their vision and plans to the team and stakeholders.

Leading a team effectively means being able to work well with others and foster a culture of collaboration. This includes being able to delegate tasks, encourage teamwork, and solve problems together.

A strong ethical foundation is essential for any leader. This includes being honest, transparent, and acting with integrity in all business dealings.

Leaders must be able to adapt to changing circumstances and pivot as needed to ensure success. A leader must be able to inspire and motivate others to work towards the common goal.

2.1 Leadership workstream activities

Mission	Communicate mission & vision to leaders & key stakeholders
Engagement	Gather inputs from leaders & business for strategy plans
verification	Verify business goals and priorities after data gathering
Strategic Plan	Create strategic plan to support business goals & priorities
Comms	Share plan for feedback and refinement
Leadership outcome	Leaders & sponsors aligned on success criteria and strategy

2.1 Leadership questions

Transformation goals	What is the goal of the digital transformation?
Problems to address	What specific problems are we trying to address?
Organisational impact	How will the transformation impact the organization's people, processes, and culture?
Technologies	What are the key technologies or platforms that will be used to support the business transformation?
Metrics	How to measure the success of the transformation?
Strategic alignment	How to ensure that the transformation is aligned with the overall business strategy and objectives?
Transformation risks	What risks and challenges to anticipate, and how will you address them?
Communications	How to communicate the transformation to stakeholders and ensure their support?
Long term success	How will you ensure that the transformation is sustainable over the long term?
Resources	What resources (financial, human, technological, etc.) will be required to support the transformation?

2.1 Leadership process

The need for change	The first step in the leadership process is to recognize that a change is necessary. This may be due to external factors such as market changes or competition, or internal factors such as inefficiencies or a need to adapt to new technologies.
Vision for the future	Develop a vision for the future. Once the need for change has been identified, leaders should develop a clear vision of what they want the organization to look like in the future. This includes setting specific goals and objectives, and outlining the steps needed to achieve them.
Communicate the vision	Leaders should clearly communicate the vision and goals to all stakeholders, including staff, customers, and investors. This helps to build support and buy-in for the transformation.
Develop a plan	Develop a plan for implementing the change. Once the vision has been established, leaders should develop a plan for how to achieve it. This may include identifying the resources needed, setting timelines, & having metrics to track progress.
Change process	Leading and managing the change process involves actively working to implement the plan and make the necessary changes such as coaching and developing staff, allocating resources, and making decisions to ensure program success.
Monitor and adjust	The leadership process does not end once the change has been implemented. Leaders should continue to monitor the progress of the transformation and make adjustments as needed so that the firm remains on track to achieve its goals.

2.1 Leadership best practices

The vision	Clearly communicate the vision and goals of the transformation to the entire organization. This helps everyone understand the reasons behind the change and how it will benefit the company.
Stakeholder engagement	Involve key stakeholders in the planning process. This helps ensure that the transformation takes into account the needs and concerns of all relevant parties.
Ongoing learning	Foster a culture of continuous learning and improvement. Encourage employees to embrace change and take an active role in shaping the transformation.
Staff informed	Keep employees informed and involved throughout the process. This helps minimize resistance to change and ensures that everyone is working towards the same goals.
Risk management	Establish a clear plan for managing and mitigating risk. Identify potential challenges and develop contingency plans to address them.
Staff empowerment	Empower employees to take ownership of their work and make decisions. This helps create a sense of ownership and commitment to the transformation.
Be agile	Stay agile and be prepared to adapt to changing circumstances. The business environment is constantly evolving, and successful transformations require leaders to be flexible and responsive.

2.1 Leadership risks

Resistance to change	It is common for employees to resist change, especially if they are comfortable with the current way of doing things. This resistance can come in the form of passive or active resistance, and it can make it difficult to implement the transformation successfully.
Cost	Business transformations can be expensive, especially if they involve significant changes to systems and processes. There is a risk that the benefits of the transformation will not outweigh the costs.
Time	Business transformations can take a long time to implement and may require a significant time investment from leaders and employees. There is a risk that the transformation will not be completed within the expected timeframe, which can result in delays and additional costs.
Goal misalignment	Misalignment with business goals: It is important for the transformation to be aligned with the overall goals and objectives of the organization. If the transformation does not support the business goals, it may not be successful.
Failure to communicate	Poor communication can lead to confusion and resistance to the transformation. It is important for leaders to clearly communicate the purpose, benefits, and expected outcomes of the transformation to all stakeholders.

2.1 Leadership lessons learned

Communications are a key success factor	Ensuring that everyone in the organization understands the goals and objectives of the transformation is critical to its success. Leaders should be clear and transparent in their communication and ensure that there are channels for employees to ask questions and provide feedback.
Focus on the customer	Business transformation should be driven by the needs of the customer, not just the needs of the business. Leaders should involve customers in the transformation process and ensure that their needs are being met.
Embrace change	Business transformation can be disruptive and can require significant changes to how the business operates. Leaders should be able to embrace change and encourage their teams to do the same.
Foster collaboration	Business transformation often requires different departments and teams to work together in new ways. Leaders should encourage collaboration and create a culture of teamwork and shared goals.
Celebrate success	Business transformation is a long and sometimes difficult process. It's important for leaders to celebrate successes along the way to keep morale high and maintain momentum.

2.2 Stakeholders

Program stakeholder management is the process of engaging with the individuals and groups who have a stake in the program or project, and ensuring that their needs and concerns are taken into account in the planning and execution of the program. This can include stakeholders within the organization, such as employees and managers, as well as external stakeholders such as customers, partners, and regulators. The goal of program stakeholder management is to ensure that the program is successful and delivers value to all stakeholders. This involves identifying and analysing stakeholder needs and expectations, and developing strategies for engaging with and addressing those needs throughout the program. It is an important aspect of project and program management, as it helps to ensure that the program is aligned with the goals and priorities of all stakeholders and that it is delivered in a way that meets their needs.

Internal stakeholders in a business transformation are individuals or groups within the organization who are directly affected by the change and have a vested interest in its success.

Each of these groups can be affected by the changes being made as part of the business transformation, and it is important to consider their needs and concerns when planning and executing the transformation. In addition, it is often helpful to involve representatives from each of these groups in the planning and decision-making process to ensure that the transformation takes their needs and perspectives into account.

External stakeholders in a business transformation are individuals or groups that are affected by, or can affect, the business, but are not directly involved in the business itself. It is important to consider the needs and concerns of external stakeholders when planning and implementing a business transformation, as their support or opposition can have a significant impact on the success of the effort.

2.2 Stakeholders workstream activities

Internal stakeholders	Identify the internal project stakeholders (PM, team, sponsor)
External stakeholders	Identify the external stakeholders (users, suppliers, external clients)
Program charter	Use the program charter to identify &record stakeholders
Feedback Meetings	Hold meetings to gain inputs & feedback (expectations, risks)
Communications	Document & share expectations, risks to all stakeholders
Stakeholders outcome	All stakeholders are identified for impact & program support

2.2 Stakeholders questions

Program charter

What are the key components of a program charter?

A program charter is a document that outlines the key components of a program. Some of the key components that are typically included in a program charter are:

- **Program mission:** The purpose and goals of the program, including the problem it aims to solve.
- **Program objectives:** Specific, measurable, achievable, relevant, and time-bound (SMART) program goals.
- **Program scope:** A description of the boundaries and limitations of the program, including the activities and deliverables that are included and excluded.
- **Program stakeholders:** A list of the individuals and groups who will be impacted by the program, or who have a vested interest in its success or failure.
- **Program team:** A list of the individuals who will be responsible for managing and executing the program, including their roles and responsibilities.
- **Program timeline:** A high-level schedule of key activities and milestones for the program (the start and end dates).
- **Program budget:** A projection of the costs associated with the program, including personnel, materials tec.
- **Program risks:** A list of potential risks and challenges that may impact the program, and a plan for addressing or mitigating those risks.
- **Program benefits:** A description of the expected benefits of the program, including how they will be measured.

2.2 Stakeholders questions

Internal stakeholders	Who are the internal stakeholders?
	• Employees are the people who work for the organization and will be most directly affected by the transformation. • Management includes upper management and executives who are responsible for overseeing and driving the transformation. • Teams and departments depending on the scope of the transformation, different teams and departments within the organization may be impacted. • If the organization is publicly traded, shareholders may also be considered internal stakeholders. • As business transformation is usually a strategic initiative, the board of directors who are responsible for overseeing the strategic direction of the organization and may be involved in decision-making related to the transformation.
External stakeholders	Who are the external stakeholders?
	Some examples of external stakeholders in a business transformation might include customers, suppliers, regulators, local communities, and advocacy groups. These stakeholders may have an interest in the success or failure of the business transformation, and may be impacted by the changes that occur as a result of the transformation.

2.2 Stakeholders process

Stakeholder management	Stakeholder management is an important part of any business transformation program, as it helps ensure that all stakeholders are informed, engaged, and aligned with the program's objectives and outcomes. By following these steps, stakeholders can be managed helping to ensure program success and the satisfaction of all stakeholders.
Stakeholders identification	The first step in stakeholder management is to identify all of the stakeholders who will be affected by the business transformation program. This may include employees, customers, suppliers, shareholders, and other groups.
Stakeholder analysis	Next, it is important to understand the interests, concerns, and influences of each stakeholder group. This will help you identify which stakeholders are most important to engage with, and how to engage with them effectively.
Stakeholder engagement plan	Based on your analysis of stakeholder interests and influences, you can develop a plan for engaging with each stakeholder group. This may include regular meetings, updates and comms channels to keep stakeholders informed.
Implement stakeholder plan	Once you have a stakeholder engagement plan in place, it is important to follow through on it. This may involve communicating with stakeholders via email, meetings, or social media.
Monitor & adjust	As the program progresses, it is important to continually monitor stakeholder engagement and adjust the stakeholder engagement plan as needed.

2.2 Stakeholders plan components

Stakeholder management plan	A stakeholder management plan is a document that outlines how a business transformation program will engage with and manage the expectations of its stakeholders.
A list of the stakeholders	This should include a list of all the individuals and groups that are affected by, or have an interest in, the program.
Stakeholder analysis	This should include an assessment of each stakeholder's level of influence and interest in the program, as well as their potential impact on its success or failure.
Stakeholder communication strategy	This should outline how the business will communicate with stakeholders about the transformation program, including the frequency and channels of communication.
Stakeholder engagement plan	his should describe how the business will involve stakeholders in the decision-making process, such as through focus groups or advisory committees.
Risk management	This should identify potential risks to the program and outline how they will be mitigated or managed.
Change management plan	This should outline how to manage the impact of the program on its staff, including training and support.
Performance measurement	This should describe how the business will track and measure the performance of the transformation program, including key performance indicators and targets.

2.2 Stakeholders risks

Resistance to change	Some stakeholders may be resistant to the changes being implemented as part of the transformation program, which can lead to delays and difficulties in executing the program.
Miscommunication	There is a risk that stakeholders may not have a clear understanding of the goals and objectives of the transformation program, which can lead to misunderstandings and misalignment.
Loss of engagement	If stakeholders are not effectively engaged in the transformation process, they may lose interest and become disengaged, which can negatively impact the success of the program.
Loss of support	If key stakeholders do not support the transformation program, it can be difficult to secure the necessary resources and support to successfully execute the program.
Negative impact on relationships	If stakeholders feel that their needs and concerns are not being adequately addressed during the transformation process, it can lead to strained relationships and potentially harm the reputation of the organization.

2.2 Stakeholders lessons learned

Identify and prioritize stakeholders	Identify and prioritize stakeholders early: It is important to identify all the stakeholders who will be impacted by the transformation program, and prioritize them based on the level of impact and the level of influence they have on the program. This will help ensure that the right stakeholders are engaged at the right time.
Communicate effectively	Clear and timely communication is key to successful stakeholder management. Make sure to keep stakeholders informed of the progress of the program, and be open and transparent about any challenges or issues that arise.
Foster collaboration	Encourage collaboration among stakeholders and try to build consensus whenever possible. This will help ensure that all stakeholders feel invested in the success of the program.
Manage expectations	Make sure to set realistic expectations with stakeholders and manage those expectations throughout the program. This will help avoid disappointment & potential conflicts down the line.
Be responsive	Be responsive to the needs and concerns of stakeholders. This will help build trust and credibility, and ensure that the program stays on track.

2.3 Communications

Effective communication is important in a business transformation program because it helps to ensure that all stakeholders are informed about the changes that are being made and understand how they will be impacted by them. It is also essential for building support and buy-in for the program, as well as for managing any potential resistance to change.

Good communication can help to minimize misunderstandings and disruptions, and can facilitate a smoother transition to the new way of doing things. Additionally, clear and open communication can help to foster a sense of transparency and trust, which is essential for building a strong and cohesive team during a time of change.

Poor communication can pose a number of risks for a business transformation program. If key stakeholders are not kept informed about the progress of the transformation program, they may not understand the direction the organization is heading and may act in ways that are misaligned with the goals of the program.

2.3 Communications workstream activities

Assessment	Assess what's going to change, why and record the case for it.
Comms plan	Create comms plan to inform & answer questions & concerns.
Comms influencers	Prepare leaders to communicate key change messages
Effect comms plan	Leaders communicate consistent messages to meet staff needs.
Comms metrics	Evaluate. the result of comms on how staff are handling change.
Communications output	The change is made visible & way to grow engagement

2.3 Communications questions

Comms Plan

What are the key components of a comms plan?

A program communication plan is a document that outlines how a program or project will communicate with its various stakeholders. Some key components of a program communication plan may include:

Objectives: This section should outline the specific goals and objectives of the program communication plan.

Audience: This section should identify the various stakeholders who will be impacted by the program or project, including internal stakeholders (such as employees) and external stakeholders.

Messages: Outline the key messages that the program or project wants to communicate to its stakeholders.

Communication channels: This section should identify the various channels that will be used to communicate with stakeholders, such as email, social media, newsletters

Timing: This section should outline the timeline for when different communication activities will take place.

Budget: This section should outline the budget allocated for communication activities, including any costs associated with using specific channels or producing materials.

Evaluation: This section should outline how the effectiveness of the program communication plan will be measured.

2.3 Communications plan components

Objectives	Identify the specific goals you want to achieve through the communications plan.
Target audience	Define the groups of people who will be affected by the transformation program and who will need to receive communication about it.
Messaging	Develop key messages that clearly and concisely describe the purpose and benefits of the transformation program.
Communication channels	Determine the most effective channels for reaching the target audience (email, newsletters, town halls, and webinars).
Timing	Plan when the different elements of the communications plan will be delivered.
Responsibilities	Assign specific roles and responsibilities for implementing the communications plan.
Budget	Establish a budget for the communications plan, including any costs for materials or external resources.
Evaluation	Develop a plan to measure the effectiveness of the communications plan and make any necessary adjustments.

2.3 Communications best practices

Clarity	It is important to be clear and concise in your communication so that your message is easily understood. Be brief and to the point, and avoid unnecessary details. Avoid using technical jargon or ambiguous language. Make sure your messages are easy to understand and free of errors.
Accuracy and honesty	Make sure the information you are communicating is accurate, honest and reliable. Choose the most appropriate way to communicate, whether that's email, or in-person.
Empathy	Try to see things from the perspective of the person you are communicating with, and be understanding of their feelings and needs. Choose a tone that is professional, respectful, and appropriate for the audience.
Feedback	Encourage feedback from the person you are communicating with, and be open to hearing and considering their thoughts and opinions. Pay attention to what the other person is saying, and show that you are listening through nonverbal cues such as nodding and maintaining eye contact. Ask for feedback on your communication style.
Be proactive	Don't wait for problems to arise, so communicate regularly and proactively to prevent misunderstandings and issues.
Document everything	Keep a record of important conversations and decisions.

2.3 Communications risks

Misunderstanding of goals	If employees are not kept informed about the goals and objectives of the transformation program, they may not understand what is expected of them or how their work fits into the larger scheme of things. This can lead to confusion and a lack of motivation.
Insufficient use of resources	Poor communication can lead to a lack of coordination among different teams and departments, resulting in the duplication of efforts and the inefficient use of resources.
Decreased productivity	Poor communication can lead to a breakdown in teamwork and collaboration, which can result in decreased productivity.
Increased resistance to change	If employees are not kept informed about the changes that are happening as part of the transformation program, they may resist those changes or be resistant to adopting new processes and technologies.
Decreased staff morale	Poor communication can lead to a lack of trust and a breakdown in relationships among employees, which can lead to decreased morale and a negative impact on the overall culture of the organization.

2.3 Communications lessons learned

General	Overall, it is important to establish clear and open channels of communication to ensure that everyone is informed and aligned throughout the business transformation program.
A lack of transparency	Poor communication can lead to a lack of transparency, which can erode trust a& create uncertainty to stakeholders.
Loss or productivity	If employees are not clear on the goals of the transformation program or how it will impact their work, they may become demotivated and less productive. This can have a negative impact on the organization's bottom line.
Staff retention	Poor communication can lead to frustration and disillusionment among employees, which may lead to an increase in turnover. This can be costly for the firm, as it may have to invest time and resources in training new employees.
Increase costs	Poor communication can lead to mistakes and rework, which can increase costs and delay the transformation process.
Reputation damage	If the transformation program is not communicated effectively, it may lead to negative perceptions among stakeholders, including customers, investors, and the general public. This can damage the organization's reputation and make it more difficult to achieve its goals.

2.4 Change Impact

Change impact refers to the effects that a change will have on the business, its employees, and its customers. In the context of a business transformation program, change impact refers to the effects that the program's changes will have on the various parts of the business.

This can include changes to processes, systems, organizational structure, and even culture. It is important to consider the potential change impact when planning a business transformation program, as it can help to identify potential challenges and opportunities, and ensure that the necessary resources are in place to support the transition.

If change impact is not considered in a business transformation program, it can lead to a number of negative consequences. For example, the change may not be fully understood or embraced by employees, which can lead to resistance and a lack of adoption.

This can in turn lead to decreased productivity, increased errors, and lower levels of customer satisfaction. The change may also not achieve its intended outcomes, as the full extent of the impact may not have been taken into account. In some cases, the change may even have unintended consequences that negatively impact the business.

Overall, not considering change impact can significantly hinder the success of a business transformation program.

2.4 Change Impact workstream activities

ASIS State	Assess the current state before the proposed change.
TOBE State	Assess the future state after the proposed change.
Gap Analysis	Determine & validate impact between ASIS and TOBE states.
Transition Needs	Sort transition needs based on impact & priority.
Design Decisions	Design decisions are based on identified impacts and needs.
Change impact outcome	The impact level is measured & plan for readiness developed.

2.4 Change Impact questions

Stakeholders impacted	Which stakeholders will be impacted by the business transformation program?
Daily work	How will this change affect the day-to-day work of staff?
Customer experience	How will this change impact the customer experience?
Training and skills	What new skills or training will employees need to successfully adapt to the change?
The bottom-line	How will the change affect the company's bottom line, either positively or negatively?
Processes & systems	Will the change require any new processes or systems to be put in place?
Partners & suppliers	How will the change impact relationships with vendors or partners?
Risks & challenges	What potential risks or challenges might arise as a result of the change?
Mission & goals	How will the change affect the company's overall mission and goals?

2.4 Change Impact plan components

General overview	A change impact plan is a key component of a business transformation program, as it helps to identify and assess the potential impacts of the changes being implemented on various stakeholders within the organization. It also outlines the strategies and actions that will be taken to minimize negative impacts and maximize positive ones.
A list of the changes	A list of the specific changes being implemented, including a description of how they will be implemented and the timeline.
Analysis of the impacts	An analysis of the potential impacts of the changes on various stakeholders within the organization, including employees, customers, and business partners.
Communications plan	A communication plan outlining how the changes will be communicated to different stakeholders and how feedback will be solicited and incorporated into the change process.
Training plan	A training plan to ensure that all relevant employees have the necessary skills and knowledge to support the changes being implemented.
Risk assessment	A risk assessment to identify and mitigate any potential risks associated with the changes.
Action plan	An action plan outlining the specific steps that will be taken to implement the changes, including any necessary resources, budgets, and timelines.

2.4 Change Impact best practices

Change impact process

The process for managing change impact in a business transformation program typically involves several steps:

- **Identify the stakeholders affected by the change:** This includes employees, customers, partners, and any other groups that will be impacted by the transformation.

- **Assess the impact of the change on each stakeholder group:** Consider how the change will affect each group's work, responsibilities, and overall experience.

- **Develop a communication and training plan:** Communicate the change to stakeholders in a clear and transparent manner, and provide necessary training to help them adjust to the new way of working.

- **Establish a process for managing resistance to change:** It's common for people to resist change, even when it's ultimately for the better. It's important to anticipate and address any resistance, and support to help people transition to the new way of working.

- **Monitor and review the change process:** Regularly check in with stakeholders to see how they are adjusting to the change, and make any adjustments to the plan.

- **Celebrate successes:** As the transformation takes hold and stakeholders become more comfortable with the new way of working, be sure to recognize and celebrate their successes. This helps to build momentum and encourage continued progress.

2.4 Change Impact risks

General overview	Conducting a risk analysis or impact assessment is an important step in any business transformation program. It helps organizations identify potential risks and impacts associated with the change and develop strategies to mitigate or manage those risks. Failing to perform a change impact analysis can lead to a range of negative consequences that can be costly and time-consuming to address.
Unforeseen disruptions	Without understanding how a change will impact different parts of the organization, there is a risk of unintended disruptions to business operations.
Increased costs	When changes are not properly planned and coordinated, it can lead to increased costs due to the need to fix problems or make additional changes.
Stakeholder resistance	When stakeholders are not informed of the potential impacts of the transformation, they may resist the change, leading to delays or even failure of the program.
Reputational damage	If the transformation program is not well-planned and managed, it could lead to negative media attention and damage to the organization's reputation.
Regulatory risks	unless the impact assessment is thorough, there is a risk of non-compliance with legal and regulatory requirements, which could lead to fines or other penalties.
Decreased customer satisfaction	If a change negatively impacts the customer experience, it can lead to decreased customer satisfaction and potentially even lead to the loss of customers.

2.4 Change Impact lessons learned

Unknown impact on stakeholders	The potential impact of the transformation program on different stakeholders, including employees, customers, and shareholders.
Unknown impact on processes and systems	The potential impact on key business processes and systems, and the need for any changes or updates to accommodate the transformation program.
Unknown impact on firm's strategy	The potential impact on the organization's overall strategy and long-term goals.
Unknown potential costs and benefits	The potential costs and benefits of the transformation program, and the potential return on investment.
Unknown potential risks and challenges	The potential risks and challenges associated with the transformation program, and the steps that can be taken to mitigate those risks.
Decreased customer satisfaction	If a change negatively impacts the customer experience, it can lead to decreased customer satisfaction and potentially even lead to the loss of customers.

2.5 Training

Business transformation programs often involve significant changes to a company's business processes, organizational structure, and/or technology systems. In order to ensure that employees are able to effectively carry out their roles within the transformed business, it may be necessary to provide them with training on new systems, tools, and processes.

This can include both technical training on specific software or hardware and more general training on how to work within the new business model. It may also be necessary to provide leadership training to help managers and executives understand how to lead and motivate their teams in the new environment.

Ultimately, the specific training requirements for a business transformation program will depend on the nature of the changes being made and the roles and responsibilities of the individuals affected by the transformation.

Training is important for the success of such programs because it helps employees understand and adapt to these changes, which can be complex and challenging.

Effective training ensures that employees have the skills and knowledge they need to perform their jobs effectively in the new business environment. It can also help to build support for the transformation program among employees and improve their engagement and commitment to the process.

Without proper training, employees may struggle to understand and implement the changes, leading to decreased productivity and potential errors. This can ultimately hinder the success of the transformation program.

2.5 Training workstream activities

Assessment	Assessing needs and resources available to meet training needs.
Motivation	Identify incentives for leaders & staff to attend training.
Training design	Plan training fit for purpose to the target audience.
Deliver training	Clearly communicate goals, objectives, and outcomes to learners.
Evaluate training	Evaluation success of training and ides for improvement.
Training outcome	The competencies required are built into the training plan.

2.5 Training questions

Program goals	What are the goals of the transformation program, and how do they align with the overall business objectives?
Key stakeholders	Who are the key stakeholders in the transformation program, and how will they be impacted by the changes being implemented?
Skills & knowledge	What new skills and knowledge will be required to support the transformation program, and how will they be acquired?
Training delivery	How will the training be delivered, and how will it be customized to meet the needs of different learners?
Training metrics	How will the effectiveness of the training be measured, and how will the results be used to refine and improve the program?
Ongoing coaching	How will ongoing support and coaching be provided to ensure that the skills and knowledge acquired during the training are put into practice and sustained over the long term?

2.5 Training plan components

Objectives	Clearly define the goals and objectives of the training program, including what you hope to achieve and how the training will support the overall transformation program.
Audience	Identify the target audience for the training, including the roles and responsibilities of each group, as well as their current skill levels and knowledge.
Content	Determine what topics and skills will be covered in the training, and how they align with the overall program.
Delivery methods	Choose the most effective delivery methods for the training, such as in-person workshops, online courses, or a combination of both.
Resources	Identify the resources needed to deliver the training, including materials, facilitators, and any technology or equipment.
Evaluation	Establish methods for evaluating the effectiveness of the training, including both formative & summative assessments.
Timing	Determine the timeline for the training program, including when and how often the training will be delivered.
Budget	Allocate the necessary budget to cover the costs of the training program, including materials, facilitator fees, and any technology or equipment expenses.

2.5 Training best practices

Training goals	Clearly define the goals and objectives of the training program. This will help you focus your efforts and ensure that the training is targeted and relevant to the needs of the business.
Stakeholder inputs	Involve key stakeholders in the design and development of the training program. This will help ensure that the training addresses the needs of the business and is aligned with the overall goals and objectives of the transformation program.
Training variety	Use a variety of training methods to cater to different learning styles and preferences. This might include traditional classroom training, online courses, simulations, and hands-on exercises.
Quality training materials	Make sure the training materials are clear, concise, and easy to understand. Use real-world examples and case studies to make the training more relevant and engaging
Ongoing support	Provide ongoing support and reinforcement to ensure that the skills and knowledge learned during the training are retained and put into practice.
Training measurement	Regularly assess the effectiveness of the training program to identify any areas that need improvement.

2.5 Training risks

Resistance to change	If employees are not included in the training process, they may be less likely to embrace the changes being implemented. This can lead to resistance to the transformation, which can be a big barrier to its success.
Decreased efficiency	Without proper training, employees may not fully understand how to use new processes or technologies, which can lead to a decrease in efficiency and an increase in the time it takes to complete tasks.
Increased errors and mistakes	Without proper training, employees may not fully understand how to use new processes or technologies, which can lead to an increase in errors and mistakes. This can result in costly rework and may damage the company's reputation.
Customer satisfaction	If employees are not trained on the new systems and processes, it could lead to issues with customer service, which could result in decreased customer satisfaction. This could ultimately lead to a decline in business.
Legal & compliance issues	If employees are not properly trained on new processes or technologies, it may increase the risk of legal and compliance issues. For example, if employees are not properly trained on data protection protocols, it may increase the risk of data breaches.

2.5 Training lessons learned

Poor adoption	Without proper training, employees may not fully understand how to use the new tools, processes, or systems being implemented as part of the transformation. This can lead to poor adoption and a failure to realize the intended benefits of the transformation.
Resistance to change	Without training, employees may feel uncertain or uncomfortable with the changes being implemented. This can lead to resistance to the transformation and make it more difficult to achieve the desired outcomes.
Employee turnover	If employees feel unprepared or unsupported during a transformation, they may become disengaged and consider leaving the company. High employee turnover can be costly and disruptive to the organization.
Decreased productivity	If employees are not properly trained, they may make mistakes or have difficulty using the new systems, which can lead to decreased productivity.
Decreased morale	A lack of training can lead to frustration and confusion among employees, which can ultimately lead to decreased morale.
Increased costs	Providing training after the fact can be more expensive and time-consuming than incorporating training into the transformation process from the start.

THE MORE THINGS CHANGE, THE MORE
THEY STAY THE SAME.

Jean-Baptiste Alphonse Karr

3.0 Process

Business processes are important in a business transformation program because they help to define how work is done within an organization. They provide a clear understanding of what needs to be done, by whom, and in what order. This helps to ensure that work is completed efficiently and effectively, and that all necessary tasks are accounted for.

Additionally, well-defined business processes can help to improve communication and coordination within an organization, as they provide a shared understanding of how work should be completed. By focusing on business processes as part of a business transformation program, organizations can streamline and optimize their operations, leading to improved performance and outcomes.

If business processes are not changed as part of a business transformation program, it is likely that the desired outcomes of the program will not be achieved. Business transformation programs are often implemented to improve efficiency, effectiveness, and competitiveness, and changing business processes is often a key element of these programs.

By not changing business processes, it is difficult to realize the benefits of the program and the organization may continue to struggle with the same challenges it was trying to address through the transformation. It is important to carefully assess and understand current business processes, identify areas for improvement, and implement changes as part of a business transformation program in order to achieve the desired results.

3.0 Process Plan Linkages

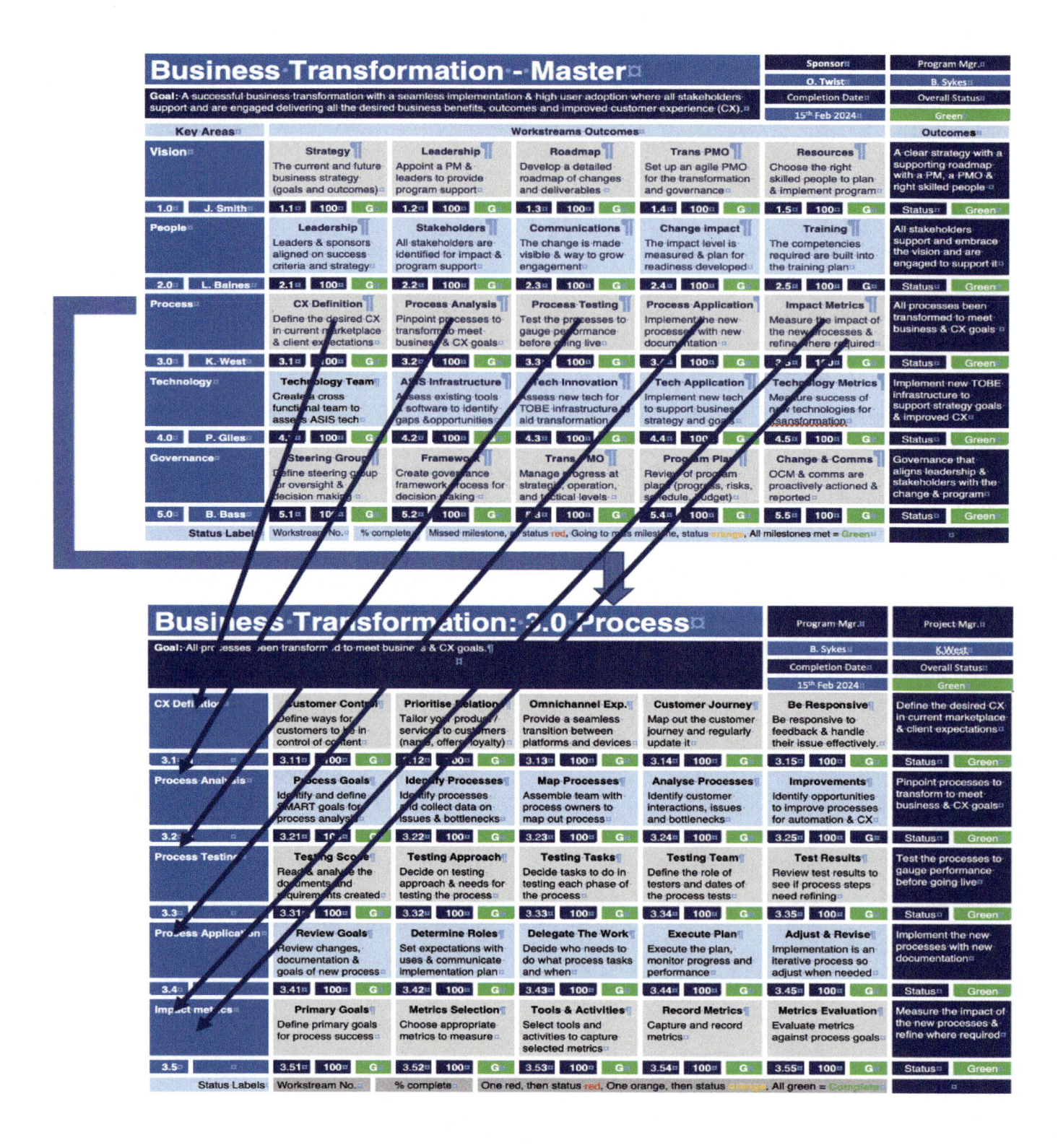

Business Transformation - Master

Sponsor: O. Twist
Program Mgr: B. Sykes
Completion Date: 15th Feb 2024
Overall Status: Green

Goal: A successful business transformation with a seamless implementation & high user adoption where all stakeholders support and are engaged delivering all the desired business benefits, outcomes and improved customer experience (CX).

Key Areas	Workstreams					Outcomes
Vision	**Strategy** — The current and future business strategy (goals and outcomes)	**Leadership** — Appoint a PM & leaders to provide program support	**Roadmap** — Develop a detailed roadmap of changes and deliverables	**Trans PMO** — Set up an agile PMO for the transformation and governance	**Resources** — Choose the right skilled people to plan & implement program	A clear strategy with a supporting roadmap with a PM, a PMO & right skilled people
1.0 J. Smith	1.1 100 G	1.2 100 G	1.3 100 G	1.4 100 G	1.5 100 G	Status Green
People	**Leadership** — Leaders & sponsors aligned on success criteria and strategy	**Stakeholders** — All stakeholders are identified for impact & program support	**Communications** — The change is made visible & way to grow engagement	**Change impact** — The impact level is measured & plan for readiness developed	**Training** — The competencies required are built into the training plan	All stakeholders support and embrace the vision and are engaged to support it
2.0 L. Baines	2.1 100 G	2.2 100 G	2.3 100 G	2.4 100 G	2.5 100 G	Status Green
Process	**CX Definition** — Define the desired CX in current marketplace & client expectations	**Process Analysis** — Pinpoint processes to transform to meet business & CX goals	**Process Testing** — Test the processes to gauge performance before going live	**Process Application** — Implement the new processes with new documentation	**Impact Metrics** — Measure the impact of the new processes & refine where required	All processes been transformed to meet business & CX goals
3.0 K. West	3.1 100 G	3.2 100 G	3.3 100 G	3.4 100 G	3.5 100 G	Status Green
Technology	**Technology Team** — Create a cross functional team to assess ASIS tech	**ASIS Infrastructure** — Assess existing tools & software to identify gaps & opportunities	**Tech Innovation** — Assess new tech for TOBE infrastructure to aid transformation	**Tech Application** — Implement new tech to support business strategy and goals	**Technology Metrics** — Measure success of new technologies for transformation	Implement new TOBE infrastructure to support strategy goals & improved CX
4.0 P. Giles	4.1 100 G	4.2 100 G	4.3 100 G	4.4 100 G	4.5 100 G	Status Green
Governance	**Steering Group** — Define steering group for oversight & decision making	**Framework** — Create governance framework process for decision making	**Trans PMO** — Manage progress at strategic, operation, and tactical levels	**Program Plan** — Review of program plan (progress, risks, schedule, budget)	**Change & Comms** — OCM & comms are proactively actioned & reported	Governance that aligns leadership & stakeholders with the change & program
5.0 B. Bass	5.1 100 G	5.2 100 G	5.3 100 G	5.4 100 G	5.5 100 G	Status Green

Status Labels: Workstream No., % complete, Missed milestone, status red, Going to miss milestone, status orange, All milestones met = Green

---

Business Transformation: 3.0 Process

Program Mgr: B. Sykes
Project Mgr: K. West
Completion Date: 15th Feb 2024
Overall Status: Green

Goal: All processes been transformed to meet business & CX goals.

	Workstreams					Outcomes
CX Definition	**Customer Control** — Define ways for customers to be in control of content	**Prioritise Relations** — Tailor your products/services to customers (name, offers, loyalty)	**Omnichannel Exp.** — Provide a seamless transition between platforms and devices	**Customer Journey** — Map out the customer journey and regularly update it	**Be Responsive** — Be responsive to feedback & handle their issue effectively.	Define the desired CX in current marketplace & client expectations
3.1	3.11 100 G	3.12 100 G	3.13 100 G	3.14 100 G	3.15 100 G	Status Green
Process Analysis	**Process Goals** — Identify and define SMART goals for process analysis	**Identify Processes** — Identify processes and collect data on issues & bottlenecks	**Map Processes** — Assemble team with process owners to map out process	**Analyse Processes** — Identify customer interactions, issues and bottlenecks	**Improvements** — Identify opportunities to improve processes for automation & CX	Pinpoint processes to transform to meet business & CX goals
3.2	3.21 100 G	3.22 100 G	3.23 100 G	3.24 100 G	3.25 100 G	Status Green
Process Testing	**Testing Scope** — Read & analyse the documents and requirements created	**Testing Approach** — Decide on testing approach & needs for testing the process	**Testing Tasks** — Decide tasks to do in testing each phase of the process	**Testing Team** — Define the role of testers and dates of the process tests	**Test Results** — Review test results to see if process steps need refining	Test the processes to gauge performance before going live
3.3	3.31 100 G	3.32 100 G	3.33 100 G	3.34 100 G	3.35 100 G	Status Green
Process Application	**Review Goals** — Review changes, documentation & goals of new process	**Determine Roles** — Set expectations with uses & communicate implementation plan	**Delegate The Work** — Decide who needs to do what process tasks and when	**Execute Plan** — Execute the plan, monitor progress and performance	**Adjust & Revise** — Implementation is an iterative process so adjust when needed	Implement the new processes with new documentation
3.4	3.41 100 G	3.42 100 G	3.43 100 G	3.44 100 G	3.45 100 G	Status Green
Impact metrics	**Primary Goals** — Define primary goals for process success	**Metrics Selection** — Choose appropriate metrics to measure	**Tools & Activities** — Select tools and activities to capture selected metrics	**Record Metrics** — Capture and record metrics	**Metrics Evaluation** — Evaluate metrics against process goals	Measure the impact of the new processes & refine where required
3.5	3.51 100 G	3.52 100 G	3.53 100 G	3.54 100 G	3.55 100 G	Status Green

Status Labels: Workstream No., % complete, One red, then status red, One orange, then status orange, All green = Complete

The Transformation Playbook

3.0 Process Workstream Plan

Business Transformation: 3.0 Process

Goal: All processes been transformed to meet business & CX goals.

		Program Mgr.	Project Mgr.
		B. Sykes	K. West
		Completion	Overall Status
		15th Feb 2024	Green

CX Definition (3.1)	**Customer** — Define ways for customers to be in control of content	**Relations** — Tailor your product / services to customers (name, offers, loyalty)	**Omnichannel** — Provide a seamless transition between platforms and devices	**CX Journey** — Map out the customer journey and regularly update it	**Responsiveness** — Be responsive to feedback & handle their issue effectively.	Define the desired CX in current marketplace & client expectations
	3.11 / 100 / G	3.12 / 100 / G	3.13 / 100 / G	3.14 / 100 / G	3.15 / 100 / G	Status: Green
Process Analysis (3.2)	**Process Goals** — Identify and define SMART goals for process analysis	**Processes** — Identify processes and collect data on issues & bottlenecks	**Map Processes** — Assemble team with process owners to map out process	**Process Analysis** — Identify customer interactions, issues and bottlenecks	**Improvements** — Identify opportunities to improve processes for automation & CX	Pinpoint processes to transform to meet business & CX goals
	3.21 / 100 / G	3.22 / 100 / G	3.23 / 100 / G	3.24 / 100 / G	3.25 / 100 / G	Status: Green
Process Testing (3.3)	**Testing Scope** — Read & analyse the documents and requirements created	**Testing Approach** — Decide on testing approach & needs for testing the process	**Testing Tasks** — Decide tasks to do in testing each phase of the process	**Testing Team** — Define the role of testers and dates of the process tests	**Test Results** — Review test results to see if process steps need refining	Test the processes to gauge performance before going live
	3.31 / 100 / G	3.32 / 100 / G	3.33 / 100 / G	3.34 / 100 / G	3.35 / 100 / G	Status: Green
Process Application (3.4)	**Review Goals** — Review changes, documentation & goals of new process	**Determine Roles** — Set expectations with uses & communicate implementation plan	**Delegation** — Decide who needs to do what process tasks and when	**Execute Plan** — Execute the plan, monitor progress and performance	**Adjust & Revise** — Implementation is an iterative process so adjust when needed	Implement the new processes with new documentation
	3.41 / 100 / G	3.42 / 100 / G	3.43 / 100 / G	3.44 / 100 / G	3.45 / 100 / G	Status: Green
Process metrics (3.5)	**Primary Goals** — Define primary goals for process success	**Metrics Selection** — Choose appropriate metrics to measure	**Tools** — Select tools and activities to capture selected metrics	**Record Metrics** — Capture and record metrics	**Evaluation** — Evaluate metrics against process goals	Measure the impact of the new processes & refine where required
	3.51 / 100 / G	3.52 / 100 / G	3.53 / 100 / G	3.54 / 100 / G	3.55 / 100 / G	Status: Green

Status Labels | Workstream No. | % complete | One red, then status red, One orange, then status orange. All green = Complete

3.1 CX Definition

Customer experience is the overall experience of a customer when interacting with a company or organization. It includes all the interactions a customer has with a company, from the initial contact or inquiry, to the purchase process, and to post-purchase follow-up.

Customer experience can be positive or negative, and it can have a significant impact on whether a customer continues to do business with a company or organization. Companies and organizations often strive to improve the customer experience in order to retain customers and attract new ones.

The customer journey is the series of interactions that a customer has with a company, from the moment they become aware of the company's products or services to the moment they make a purchase and beyond. This journey can include many different touchpoints, such as visiting the company's website, reading reviews, visiting a physical store, interacting with customer service, and more.

The goal of the customer journey is to understand the steps that a customer goes through in order to make a purchase, and to optimize each step in the journey to make it as easy and enjoyable as possible for the customer.

3.1 CX definition workstream activities

Customer control	Define ways for customers to be in control of content
Prioritise relations	Tailor your product / services to customers (name, offers, loyalty)
Omnichannel	Provide a seamless transition between platforms and devices
Customer journey	Map out the customer journey and regularly update it
Responsiveness	Be responsive to feedback & handle their issue effectively.
CX definition outcome	Define the desired CX in current marketplace & client expectations

3.1 CX definition questions

Touchpoints	**What are the different touchpoints that customers have with the company?**
	This includes all the ways in which customers interact with the company, such as visiting the website, calling customer service, or visiting a physical store.
Customer perception	**How do customers feel at each touchpoint?**
	This involves understanding the emotions that customers experience at each touchpoint, as well as any pain points or frustrations they may have.
Customer interactions	**What actions do customers take at each touchpoint?**
	Understanding the actions that customers take at each touchpoint can help you identify any barriers or roadblocks that may be preventing them from achieving their goals.
Customer journey differences	**How does the customer journey differ for different customer segments?**
	It can be helpful to analyse the customer experience and journey for different segments of customers, such as new versus returning customers, or customers in different geographic regions.
Customer journey over time	**How does the customer journey evolve over time?**
	It's important to track the customer journey over time to understand how it changes and evolves, and to identify any trends or patterns that emerge.

3.1 CX plan components

General overview	A customer experience plan is a strategic document that outlines how a business intends to improve the customer experience at every touchpoint.
Customer journey map	A visual map of the steps a customer takes while interacting with a firm, from awareness to purchase and beyond.
Customer personas	Detailed profiles of the business's typical customers, including their needs, behaviours, and preferences.
Customer pain points	A list of the problems or challenges that customers face while interacting with the business.
Service standards	A set of guidelines for how employees should treat customers and respond to their needs.
Customer feedback mechanisms	A system for collecting and analysing customer feedback, such as surveys or focus groups.
Service recovery plan	A plan for how to handle and resolve customer complaints.
Training and development	A program for training employees on how to deliver excellent customer service and address customer pain points.
Metrics and KPIs	A set of measurable goals for improving the customer experience, along with a plan for tracking progress towards these goals.

3.1 CX definition best practices

Multiple contact points	Make it easy for customers to reach out to you. Provide multiple channels for customers to get in touch, such as email, phone, and social media.
Quick responses	Respond quickly to customer inquiries. Customers appreciate timely responses, so make sure to address their concerns as soon as possible.
Show empathy	Customers are more likely to have a positive experience if they feel like you understand and care about their needs.
Keep customers informed	Keep customers up-to-date on the status of their orders, and let them know if there are any delays or issues
Solve problems	Solve problems efficiently, if a customer has a problem, try to resolve it as quickly and effectively as possible.
Follow-up after sales	Follow up with customers, after a purchase or customer service interaction, follow up to make sure that the customer is satisfied & see if there is anything else you can do to help.
Customer feedback	Seek customer feedback from customers to understand how to improve their experience.

3.1 CX definition risks

General overview	Overall, defining customer experience is an important aspect of any business transformation as it helps ensure that your efforts are aligned with the needs and expectations of your customers, and that you are able to deliver a positive experience that meets or exceeds their expectations.
Poor customer satisfaction	If you don't have a clear understanding of what your customers expect from your business, you may not be able to deliver a positive customer experience. This can lead to low customer satisfaction and potentially result in lost business.
Decreased efficiency	Without a clear understanding of customer needs and preferences, it may be more difficult to streamline processes and optimize resources. This can lead to decreased efficiency and increased costs.
Difficulty adapting to change	If you don't have a clear understanding of your customer experience, it may be more difficult to anticipate and respond to changes in the market or customer preferences. This can lead to a lack of agility and competitiveness.
Difficulty measuring success	Without a clear understanding of customer experience, it may be difficult to determine if your business transformation is successful or not. You won't have a clear way to measure the impact of your efforts on customer satisfaction and loyalty.

3.1 CX definition lessons learned

Reputational damage	If a business transformation negatively impacts the customer experience, it can damage the company's reputation. This can be particularly damaging if the transformation is widely publicized, as it can lead to negative press and a loss of trust from customers and other stakeholders.
Customer churn	If customers are unhappy with their experience, they may choose to take their business elsewhere. This can lead to a high churn rate and reduced customer loyalty.
Transformation may fail	If a business transformation does not take into account the customer experience, it is less likely to achieve its desired goals such as increasing customer loyalty, improving customer satisfaction, or driving revenue growth.
Customer feedback	By listening to and responding to customer feedback, companies can identify and address issues that are causing poor customer experiences.
The value of empathy	Putting yourself in the customer's shoes can help companies understand and address their needs and concerns.
Ongoing improvement	Companies have learned the marketplace does not stand still and the need for continuous improvement: Companies should be proactive in seeking out ways to improve the customer experience, rather than waiting for problems to arise.
Focus on the customer	The importance of having a customer-centric culture: A company-wide focus on the customer experience can help ensure that all employees are committed to delivering a positive experience.

3.2 Process Analysis

Business process analysis is the practice of examining a business process in order to understand it fully, identify any inefficiencies or problems, and recommend ways to improve it. It involves examining the steps involved in a process, the inputs and outputs of each step, and the people and resources involved.

The goal of business process analysis is to improve the efficiency and effectiveness of the process, and to identify opportunities for automation or other improvements. This can be done through a variety of techniques, including process mapping, process modelling, and process simulation.

Not doing process analysis as part of a business transformation program can have several negative impacts.

First, it can lead to a lack of understanding of how the current processes work, which can make it difficult to identify problems or inefficiencies that need to be addressed. This can result in the implementation of solutions that are not effective, or that may even cause new problems.

Second, not doing process analysis can also lead to a lack of buy-in from employees who may be asked to change their work processes as part of the transformation. Without understanding the reasons for the changes or how they will benefit the organization, employees may be resistant to the changes and may not fully adopt the new processes.

Finally, not doing process analysis can also hinder the overall success of the business transformation program. Without a clear understanding of the current processes, it can be difficult to set clear goals and objectives for the transformation, and to measure the success of the program.

3.2 Process analysis workstream activities

Process goals	Identify and define SMART goals for process analysis.
Identify processes	Identify processes and collect data on issues & bottlenecks.
Map processes	Assemble team with process owners to map out process.
Analyse processes	Identify customer interactions, issues and bottlenecks.
Improvements	Identify opportunities to improve processes for automation & CX.
Process analysis outcome	Pinpoint processes to transform to meet business & CX goals.

3.2 Process analysis questions

Target process name & owner	What is the current process, who owns it and how is it being carried out?
Process goals	What are the goals of the process and how well is it achieving them?
Process inputs & outputs	What are the inputs and outputs of the process?
Process roles & responsibilities	Who is involved in the process and what are their roles and responsibilities?
Process bottlenecks	Are there any bottlenecks or inefficiencies in the process?
Process costs	What are the costs associated with the process?
Business strategy	How does the process fit within the overall business strategy?
Regulatory needs	Are there any regulatory or compliance requirements that must be considered in the process?
Process risks	What are the potential risks associated with the process?
Opportunities	What are the potential opportunities for improving the process?

3.2 Process analysis plan components

General overview	A process analysis plan is a tool used to understand and improve business processes. It is a systematic approach to identifying and analysing the steps involved in a process, with the goal of making the process more efficient and effective.
Scope of the process	Identify the boundaries of the process being analysed and define the specific goals of the process analysis.
Process stakeholders	Identify the people or groups who are directly or indirectly impacted by the process, and who have a role in the process.
Map the process	Document the steps involved in the process using a visual tool, including inputs, outputs, and any decision points.
Analyse the process	Identify areas of the process that are inefficient, redundant, or unnecessary. Look for opportunities to streamline the process and eliminate waste.
Identify solutions	Develop and prioritize potential solutions to improve the process. Consider the costs, benefits & risks of each solution.
Implement & test	Select the most promising solutions and implement them in a controlled manner, monitoring their effectiveness and making any necessary adjustments.
Review and revise	Regularly review the process to ensure that it is still meeting the needs of the business and make any necessary revisions.

3.2 Process analysis best practices

Process analysis scope	Clearly define the scope of the process analysis. Determine the specific business processes that will be analysed and why they are being targeted for transformation.
Involve key stakeholders	Ensure that the people who are responsible for the processes being analysed are involved in the process analysis. This will help ensure that the analysis is accurate and that the inputs for improvement are feasible and supported.
A structured approach	There are many different methodologies that can be used to analyse business processes. Some common ones include Six Sigma, Lean, and the Business Process Modelling Notation (BPMN). Whichever methodology is used, it is important to follow a structured approach to ensure that the analysis is thorough and consistent.
The ASIS process	Document the current state of the process, It is important to have a clear understanding of how the process currently works before attempting to transform it. This includes documenting the steps involved in the process, the resources (people, systems, etc.) that are required, and any bottlenecks or inefficiencies that exist.

3.2 Process analysis best practices

Improvement opportunities	Identify opportunities for improvement. Once the current state of the process has been documented, the next step is to identify areas where the process could be improved. This might include streamlining steps, eliminating unnecessary activities, or automating tasks.
The TOBE process	Design the future state of the process. Based on the opportunities for improvement that have been identified, design a new version of the process that is more efficient and effective. This should include a detailed description of the steps involved, as well as any new resources that will be required.
Communicate the plan	It is important to communicate the plan for transforming the process to all stakeholders, including those who will be responsible for implementing the changes. This will help ensure that everyone is on board and aware of what needs to be done.
Implement & monitor	Implement and monitor the changes: Once the plan has been developed and communicated, the final step is to implement the changes and monitor their effectiveness. This may involve making further adjustments as needed to ensure that the transformed process is working as intended.

3.2 Process analysis risks

General overview	Overall, not doing a process analysis before implementing a business transformation can lead to a number of negative outcomes, including decreased productivity, increased costs, and decreased customer satisfaction.
Inefficient processes	Without understanding the current processes, it is difficult to determine how to improve them. As a result, the transformation may result in processes that are still inefficient or even less efficient than before.
Decreased productivity	If the transformation does not take into account the needs of the employees who will be using the new processes, it can lead to decreased productivity as they struggle to adapt to the changes.
Increased costs	If the transformation does not address underlying issues with the current processes, it may actually end up increasing costs rather than reducing them.
Decreased customer satisfaction	If the transformation does not consider the needs of the customers, it can lead to decreased satisfaction and potentially even lost business.
Incomplete or inaccurate data	Another risk is that the data used to inform the process analysis may be incomplete or inaccurate. This can lead to flawed conclusions and recommendations, which can have serious consequences for the business.

3.2 Process analysis lessons learned

Resistance to change	A lesson learned is that employees may resist the changes being proposed. This can be due to a variety of factors, including a lack of understanding of the benefits of the changes, fear of the unknown, or a lack of trust in the leadership team.
Misalignment with business goals	The changes being proposed as part of the business transformation may not be aligned with the overall goals and objectives of the organization. This can lead to confusion and frustration among employees, and ultimately result in the transformation efforts failing.
Stakeholder involvement	It is important lesson learned to involve all relevant stakeholders in the process analysis and decision-making process. This will help to ensure that the changes being proposed are aligned with the needs and goals of the organization, and that there is buy-in from all parties.
Ensure analysis is thorough	Following a structured approach, such as the Lean Six Sigma methodology, can help to ensure that the process analysis is thorough and comprehensive.
Communicate clearly	A key lesson learned is that clear and open communication is key to the success of any business transformation. It is important to keep employees informed about the changes being proposed and to be transparent about the reasons

3.3 Process Testing

Business process testing is a type of testing that is performed on business processes to ensure that they are working correctly and efficiently. This is typically done as part of a business transformation program, where the goal is to improve the efficiency and effectiveness of business processes by identifying and fixing any issues or bottlenecks.

During business process testing, a series of tests are designed and executed to validate the correctness, completeness, and quality of the business processes. These tests may be manual or automated, and may involve simulating different scenarios and user actions to ensure that the process is functioning as intended.

The goal of business process testing is to identify any problems or issues with the business process, and to recommend changes or improvements to enhance the process. This can involve redesigning the process, introducing new technologies or tools, or making other changes to streamline the process and improve efficiency.

Not performing business process testing during a business transformation program can lead to a number of risks, including:

- Without testing, it is difficult to determine whether the new processes are more efficient than the old ones. This can lead to wasted time and resources.
- If the new processes are not intuitive or do not meet the needs of the users, they may be poorly adopted. This can result in reduced productivity and employee dissatisfaction.
- If the new processes are not tested and optimized, they may require more resources (e.g., time, money, personnel) to complete, resulting in increased costs for the organization.
- If the new processes are not effective, it can lead to a decline in the quality of products or services, which can result in a loss of revenue.
- If the business transformation program is not successful, it can damage the reputation of the organization and make it difficult to attract and retain customers.

3.3 Process testing workstream activities

Testing scope	Read & analyse the documents and requirements created.
Testing approach	Decide on testing approach & needs for testing the process.
Testing tasks	Decide tasks to do in testing each phase of the process.
Testing team	Define the role of testers and dates of the process tests.
Test results	Review test results to see if process steps need refining.
Process testing outcome	Test the processes to gauge performance before going live.

3.3 Process testing questions

Goal alignment	Is the business process being tested aligned with the overall goals and objectives of the transformation program?
Desired state	Does the new business process accurately reflect the desired state of the firm, its systems, processes, and people?
Process efficiency	Is the business process efficient and effective in meeting the needs of customers and stakeholders?
Bottlenecks	Are there any bottlenecks or inefficiencies in the business process testing that need to be addressed?
Compliance	Does the business process comply with relevant laws, regulations, and industry standards?
Process documentation	Is the business process adequately documented and understood by the people who will be executing it?
Process scalability	Is the business process scalable to accommodate growth?
Process resources	Have the necessary resources been allocated to support the business process, including people, technology, and budget?
Risks & impacts	Have the potential risks and impacts of the business process been identified and addressed?
Process monitoring	How will the business process be monitored and measured to ensure it is meeting its intended goals?

3.3 Process testing plan components

Objectives	Clearly define the goals and objectives of the testing process. What you are hoping to achieve and why it is important.
Scope	Identify the scope of the testing process, including which processes will be tested and any constraints or limitations that may impact the testing.
Approach	Determine the approach that will be used for testing, including whether you will use manual or automated testing techniques and any tools that will be used.
Test cases	Identify the specific test cases that will be executed during the testing process, including the steps that need to be followed and the expected outcomes.
Test data	Determine the data that will be used for testing, including how it will be prepared and any specific requirements.
Test environment	Specify the environment in which the testing will be conducted (hardware, software, infrastructure requirements).
Testing resources	Identify the resources that will be needed for the testing process (personnel, equipment, and any other materials).
Testing schedule	Develop a timeline for the testing process, including any milestones or deadlines that need to be met.
Reporting	Determine how test results will be reported and to whom they will be communicated.
Risks & contingencies	Identify any potential risks or issues that may arise during the testing process, develop contingency plans to address them.

3.3 Process testing best practices

Program goals	Clearly define the goals and objectives of the business transformation program, as well as the expected outcomes of the new processes.
Key stakeholders	Identify the key stakeholders who will be impacted by the new processes, and involve them in the testing process.
Process test plan	Develop a testing plan that outlines the scope, approach, and resources required for the testing.
Testing techniques	Use a variety of testing techniques, such as manual testing, automated testing, and user acceptance testing, to ensure that the new processes are thoroughly tested.
Controlled environment	Conduct testing in a controlled environment, such as a test environment or a staging environment, to minimize the impact on production systems.
Document test results	Document the results of the testing, including any issues that were identified and how they were addressed.
Results for refinement	Use the results of the testing to refine and improve the new processes before they are deployed in the production area.
Process monitoring	Continuously monitor the performance of the new processes after they are deployed to ensure that they are meeting the desired outcomes.

3.3 Process testing risks

General overview	Overall, it is important to thoroughly test any new process to ensure that it is functioning as intended and to minimize the risk of errors, inefficiencies, and other issues that could impact the business.
Risk of failure	One of the main risks is that the business process changes may not work as intended, leading to a failure of the transformation program.
Risk of disruption	Business process testing can disrupt the existing business processes, leading to reduced efficiency and productivity.
Resistance to change	There may be resistance to change from employees, which can hinder the success of the transformation program.
Lack of visibility	Without process testing, you may not have a clear understanding of how the new process is functioning and whether it is meeting the desired outcomes.
Increased risk of errors	Without proper testing, it is more likely that errors and defects will be present in the new process, which can lead to costly rework and delays.
Decreased efficiency	If the new process is not thoroughly tested, it may not be as efficient as it could be, leading to reduced productivity.
Increased costs	If any of the above issues occur, it could lead to increased costs as the business works to fix problems and get the new process running smoothly.
Decreased customer satisfaction	If the new process is not functioning as intended, it could lead to a decline in customer satisfaction, which can have a negative impact on the business.

3.3 Process testing risks & lessons learned

Increased risk of project failure	Without process testing, it is difficult to identify and address potential issues before they become problems. This can increase the risk of project failure, as issues may not be discovered until it is too late to fix them.
More difficulty fixing problems	If problems are not identified and addressed during the testing phase, they may not be discovered until after the transformation has been implemented. This can make it much more difficult and costly to fix problems.
Reduce quality	Without testing, it is difficult to ensure that the transformed process is of high quality and meets the needs of the business. This can result in a not fit for purpose process.
Detailed planning	It is important to plan and design the process changes and test them before implementing them in the live environment.
Resource availability	Adequate resources, including time, budget, & staff need to be allocated for process testing to ensure its success.
Clear communications	Clear communication is essential to ensure that all impacted stakeholders understand the changes being made and how they will be affected by them.
Lost time & resources	Not conducting process testing can result in wasted time and resources, as issues may not be identified until after the transformation has been implemented. This can result in additional time and resources being required to fix problems and bring the process up to an acceptable standard.
Need for flexibility	it may be necessary to be flexible and adapt to changes as the testing process proceeds, in order to ensure the success of the transformation program.

3.4 Process Application

It's important to note that implementing a new business process can be a complex and time-consuming process, so it's important to be well-prepared and to manage the project carefully.

There are several steps to take to ensure that a new process is ready to be implemented in a production environment. After the process has been tested thoroughly in a staging or development environment to ensure it is working as intended and to identify and fix any issues.

Ensure the process is documented including any necessary input or output data, dependencies, and any special instructions or considerations. Make sure the relevant personnel are trained on the process and how to use it effectively.

A roll-out plan that needs to be developed outlining how and when the process will be introduced to the production environment, including any necessary maintenance windows or downtime.

In addition, a plan for monitoring the process should be developed after it has been implemented to ensure it is running smoothly and identify any potential issues. Also, have a contingency plan in place in case of the process experiences any issues or errors once it is live in the production environment.

3.4 Process application workstream activities

Review goals	Review changes, documentation & goals of new process.
Determine roles	Set expectations with uses & communicate implementation plan.
Delegate the work	Decide who needs to do what process tasks and when.
Execute plan	Execute the plan, monitor progress and performance.
Adjust and revise	Implementation is an iterative process so adjust when needed.
Process application outcome	Implement the new processes with new documentation.

3.4 Process application questions

Process purpose	What is the purpose of the new process?
Business outcomes	How will the new process improve business outcomes?
Required resources	What resources (people, time, money) are required to implement the new process?
Process ROI	What is the expected return on investment for implementing the new process?
Go-live approvals	Have the necessary approvals been obtained?
Execution owner	Who is responsible for implementing the new process?
Process training	What training is required for employees to use the new process effectively?
Process monitoring	How will the new process be monitored and evaluated?
Contingency plans	What contingency plans are in place in case the new process is not successful?
Process integration	How will the new process be integrated with existing processes and systems?

3.4 Process application go-live plan

Project scope & objectives	This includes a clear definition of the new process, the business problem it aims to solve, and the expected outcomes of the transformation.
Stakeholder analysis	his involves identifying all the stakeholders who will be impacted by the new process, including employees, customers, and other external partners.
Resource and budget plan	This includes an estimation of the resources (e.g., time, personnel, equipment) and budget needed to successfully implement the new process.
Communication plan	This outlines how you will communicate the changes to all stakeholders, including employees, customers, and other external partners.
Training plan	This outlines how you will provide training to employees on the new process & any new tools or systems used for it.
Change management plan	This outlines how you will manage the transition to the new process, including how to address any resistance to change.
Testing and validation plan	This outlines how you will test the new process to ensure it is working as intended before it is fully implemented.
Rollout plan	This outlines the steps for implementing the new process, including any necessary changes to systems or processes and the timeline for the rollout.
Post implementation review	This includes plans for ongoing monitoring and evaluation of the new process to ensure it is meeting the expected outcomes and making the desired impact on the business.

3.4 Process application best practices

Process goals	Clearly define the goals and objectives of the new process, and how it will benefit the business.
Risks & challenges	Identify and address potential risks and challenges that may arise during the implementation process.
Stakeholder involvement	Involve all relevant stakeholders in the planning and design of the new process.
Project plan	Develop a detailed project plan, including timelines and resources required.
Process testing	Test the new process thoroughly in a non-production environment before rolling it out to the production area
Training & support	Provide thorough training and support for employees who will be using the new process.
Process monitoring	Monitor and measure the performance of the new process, and make adjustments as needed.
Communications	Communicate effectively with all relevant parties throughout the implementation process to ensure a smooth transition.
Celebrate success	Celebrate successes and recognize the efforts of all involved in the successful implementation of the new process.

3.4 Process application risks

Resistance to change	Employees may resist the new process due to a variety of reasons such as lack of understanding or fear of the unknown. This can lead to reduced productivity and difficulty in achieving the desired results.
Cost overruns	Implementing a new process can be expensive, and there is a risk of cost overruns if the project is not properly planned and managed.
Technology issues	If the new process relies on technology, there is a risk of technical problems occurring that could disrupt the process.
Legal and regulatory risks	There is a risk of non-compliance with laws and regulations if the new process is not properly designed and implemented.
Data security	If the new process involves the handling of sensitive data, there is a risk of data breaches or other security incidents occurring.
Reputation risk	If the implementation of the new process is not successful, it could damage the company's reputation with customers, partners, and other stakeholders.

3.4 Process application lessons learned

Change management	There needs to be a clear plan for how the new process will be introduced &communicated to the relevant stakeholders.
Training and documentation	An essential best practice is to ensure that all relevant employees are trained on the new process &documentation is in place before going live in a production environment.
Testing and validation	As previously mentioned, It is important to thoroughly test the new process in a controlled environment before rolling it out to production.
Impact on existing processes	The implementation of a new process may impact existing processes and systems, so it is important to carefully assess and address any potential issues.
Data migration	Data migration is always a key are to consider if the new process involves moving data from one system to another, it is important to carefully plan and execute the data migration to avoid any loss or corruption of data.
Resource allocation	The implementation of a new process may require additional resources, so it is important to ensure that sufficient resources are available and allocated appropriately.

3.5 Process Metrics

It is important to measure the impact and performance of new business processes because it allows an organization to determine whether the changes, they have made are effective and achieving the desired outcomes. By collecting and analysing data on the performance of the new process, an organization can identify any problems or inefficiencies and make adjustments to improve the process. Additionally, measuring the performance of new business processes can help an organization to justify the resources that were invested in implementing the changes and demonstrate the value of the process to stakeholders.

There are several best practices for using metrics to measure the impact and performance of new business processes and by following best practices, you can effectively use metrics to measure the impact and performance of your new business process.

There are many key metrics that can be used to measure the impact and performance of a new business process.

Some examples of metrics that you may want to consider include:

- How much does the new process cost in terms of time, resources, and money?
- How efficiently does the new process achieve its goals?
- What is the quality of the output of the new process?
- How quickly does the new process produce results?
- How adaptable is the new process to changing circumstances and requirements?
- How well does the new process meet the needs and expectations of customers?
- Employee satisfaction: How well does the new process meet the needs and expectations of employees?
- Does the new process encourage innovation and continuous improvement?

3.5 Process metrics workstream activities

Primary goals	Define primary goals for process success.
Metrics selection	Choose appropriate metrics to measure.
Tools & activities	Select tools and activities to capture selected metrics.
Record metrics	Capture and record metrics.
Metrics evaluation	Evaluate metrics against process goal.
Process metrics outcome	Measure the impact of the new processes & refine where require.

3.5 Process metrics questions

Process goal	**What is the goal of the new business process?**
	This will help you determine which metrics are most relevant to measure its success.
Process KPIs	**What are the key performance indicators (KPIs) for the new business process?**
	These are the specific metrics that you will use to track the performance of the process.
Data collection	**How will you collect data on the KPIs?**
	This will involve determining which tools or methods you will use to gather the necessary data.
Data analysis	**How will you analyse the data?**
	This will involve deciding how you will interpret the data and determine whether the new business process is having the desired impact.
Results communications	**How will you communicate the results of the analysis?**
	This will involve deciding how you will share the results with relevant stakeholders, such as management, employees, and customers.
The use of results	**How will you use the results of the analysis to improve the new business process?**
	This will involve identifying any areas for improvement and implementing changes to optimize the process.

3.5 Process metrics best practices

Identify KPIs	Identify the key performance indicators (KPIs) that are most relevant to your business goals and objectives. These are the metrics that will help you determine whether your new business process is having the desired impact.
KPIs baseline metrics	Establish baseline measurements for your KPIs before you implement the new process. This will allow you to compare the results of the new process to the previous state of your business.
Regular collection	Collect data on your KPIs regularly and consistently. This will help you track the performance of your new business process over time and identify any trends or patterns.
Data visualization tools	Use data visualization tools to present your data in a clear and easy-to-understand way. This will help you communicate the results of your new business process to stakeholders and decision makers.
Process improvement	Use your KPI data to continuously improve your business process. Look for opportunities to optimize and streamline your process based on the data you have collected.
KPI reviews & updates	Be sure to regularly review and update your KPIs to ensure that they are still relevant & aligned with your business goals.

3.5 Process metrics risks

Relying too much on metrics	Using metrics to measure the impact and performance of new business processes can be a useful tool for identifying areas of improvement and for demonstrating the value of the process to stakeholders. One risk is that relying too heavily on metrics can lead to a focus on short-term goals at the expense of long-term strategy. This can result in "gaming the system" or finding ways to optimize the metrics rather than actually improving the process.
Wrong metrics	Another risk is that using the wrong metrics can lead to unintended consequences. For example, if a metric is chosen that does not accurately reflect the goals of the process, the process may be improved in ways that do not align with the overall objectives of the organization.
Difficult to interpret	Metrics can be difficult to interpret, especially if they are not properly designed or if they do not accurately capture the key aspects of the new process. This can lead to incorrect conclusions about the effectiveness of the process.
Metrics can be manipulated	Metrics can be subject to manipulation, either intentionally or unintentionally. This can make it difficult to trust the results, and can undermine the credibility of the process.
Metrics use can impact other goals	Using metrics to measure the success of a new process can create pressure to achieve specific targets, which can lead to unhealthy competition or a focus on achieving the metrics at the expense of other important goals.

3.5 Process metrics lessons learned

Identify the right metrics	It is important to identify the right metrics to measure the success of the new process. These process metrics should be aligned with the goals of the transformation.
Establish baseline	It is important to establish a baseline for the metrics that you will be tracking. This will provide a point of reference to compare the results of the new process to and will help you understand the impact of the changes that you have made.
Define process goals	A key lesson learned is to clearly define the goals and objectives of the process before selecting metrics.
Aligned with goals	Choose metrics that are aligned with the process goals.
A good mix of metrics	Use a mix of metrics to get a complete picture of the process.
Review metrics	To get a complete picture of the effectiveness of the new process, it is important to regularly track and monitor the metrics that you have chosen.
Metrics as a guide	Use metrics as a guide rather than a target, and be mindful of the potential risks and limitations of relying on metrics.
Use data to make informed decisions	The data that you collect from tracking the metrics should be used to inform your decision-making process. By analysing the data, you can identify trends and patterns that can help you optimize the new process and achieve better results.
Be flexible	As you track the metrics, you may discover that certain aspects of the new process are not working as well as expected. Be open to adapting and adjusting the process as needed to ensure that it is effective and aligned with the goals of the business transformation.

CHANGE IS THE ONLY THING THAT BRINGS PROGRESS.

Friedrich Nietzsche

4.0 Technology

Technology can play a number of important roles in a business transformation program. Some of the ways in which technology can support business transformation include:

- Technology can enable businesses to operate in new and more efficient ways, such as by automating manual processes or enabling new types of customer interactions.
- Technology can help to facilitate communication and collaboration within and between teams, which can be especially important when teams are geographically dispersed or working remotely.
- Technology can be used to improve the customer experience by making it easier for customers to interact with the business, such as through the use of self-service mobile apps.
- Technology can help businesses to be more agile and responsive to change, such as by enabling teams to work on projects in a more flexible and collaborative way.
- By implementing new technology, a company may be able to streamline processes and workflows, leading to increased productivity and reduced costs
- Adopting new technology can give a company an edge over competitors, particularly if the technology is cutting-edge or hard to replicate.

However, there are also some potential cons to consider:

- Implementing new technology can be expensive, particularly if it requires significant infrastructure changes or training for employees.
- Some employees may resist using new technology, particularly if they are comfortable with existing systems and processes. This can lead to reduced productivity and morale.

Relying too heavily on technology can make a company vulnerable if something goes wrong with the systems. This could be due to technological issues, such as outages or software bugs, or external factors like natural disasters or cyber-attacks.

4.0 Technology Plan Linkages

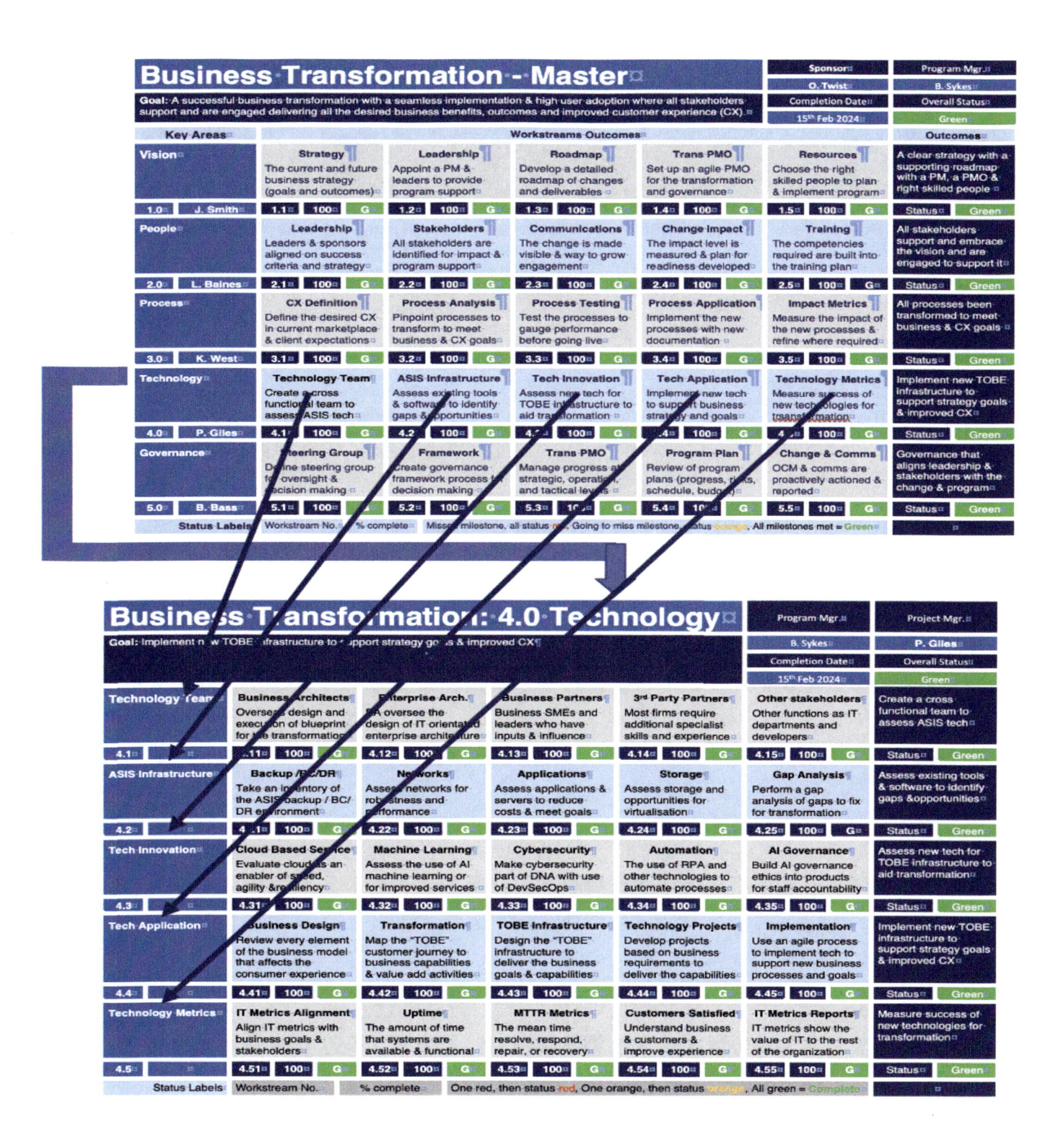

Business Transformation - Master

Sponsor: O. Twist
Program Mgr.: B. Sykes
Completion Date: 15th Feb 2024
Overall Status: Green

Goal: A successful business transformation with a seamless implementation & high user adoption where all stakeholders support and are engaged delivering all the desired business benefits, outcomes and improved customer experience (CX).

Key Areas	Workstreams					Outcomes
Vision 1.0 J. Smith	**Strategy** (1.1) The current and future business strategy (goals and outcomes) — 100 G	**Leadership** (1.2) Appoint a PM & leaders to provide program support — 100 G	**Roadmap** (1.3) Develop a detailed roadmap of changes and deliverables — 100 G	**Trans PMO** (1.4) Set up an agile PMO for the transformation and governance — 100 G	**Resources** (1.5) Choose the right skilled people to plan & implement program — 100 G	A clear strategy with a supporting roadmap with a PM, a PMO & right skilled people. Status: Green
People 2.0 L. Baines	**Leadership** (2.1) Leaders & sponsors aligned on success criteria and strategy — 100 G	**Stakeholders** (2.2) All stakeholders are identified for impact & program support — 100 G	**Communications** (2.3) The change is made visible & way to grow engagement — 100 G	**Change Impact** (2.4) The impact level is measured & plan for readiness developed — 100 G	**Training** (2.5) The competencies required are built into the training plan — 100 G	All stakeholders support and embrace the vision and are engaged to support it. Status: Green
Process 3.0 K. West	**CX Definition** (3.1) Define the desired CX in current marketplace & client expectations — 100 G	**Process Analysis** (3.2) Pinpoint processes to transform to meet business & CX goals — 100 G	**Process Testing** (3.3) Test the processes to gauge performance before going live — 100 G	**Process Application** (3.4) Implement the new processes with new documentation — 100 G	**Impact Metrics** (3.5) Measure the impact of the new processes & refine where required — 100 G	All processes been transformed to meet business & CX goals. Status: Green
Technology 4.0 P. Giles	**Technology Team** (4.1) Create a cross functional team to assess ASIS tech — 100 G	**ASIS Infrastructure** (4.2) Assess existing tools & software to identify gaps & opportunities — 100 G	**Tech Innovation** (4.3) Assess new tech for TOBE infrastructure to aid transformation — 100 G	**Tech Application** (4.4) Implement new tech to support business strategy and goals — 100 G	**Technology Metrics** (4.5) Measure success of new technologies for transformation — 100 G	Implement new TOBE infrastructure to support strategy goals & improved CX. Status: Green
Governance 5.0 B. Bass	**Steering Group** (5.1) Define steering group for oversight & decision making — 100 G	**Framework** (5.2) Create governance framework process for decision making — 100 G	**Trans PMO** (5.3) Manage progress at strategic, operational, and tactical levels — 100 G	**Program Plan** (5.4) Review of program plans (progress, risks, schedule, budget) — 100 G	**Change & Comms** (5.5) OCM & comms are proactively actioned & reported — 100 G	Governance that aligns leadership & stakeholders with the change & program. Status: Green

Status Labels: Workstream No. | % complete | Missed milestone, all status red, Going to miss milestone, status orange, All milestones met = Green

---

Business Transformation: 4.0 Technology

Program Mgr.: B. Sykes
Project Mgr.: P. Giles
Completion Date: 15th Feb 2024
Overall Status: Green

Goal: Implement new TOBE infrastructure to support strategy goals & improved CX

	Workstreams					Outcomes
Technology Team 4.1	**Business Architects** (4.11) Oversee design and execution of blueprint for the transformation — 100 G	**Enterprise Arch.** (4.12) PA oversee the design of IT orientated enterprise architecture — 100 G	**Business Partners** (4.13) Business SMEs and leaders who have inputs & influence — 100 G	**3rd Party Partners** (4.14) Most firms require additional specialist skills and experience — 100 G	**Other stakeholders** (4.15) Other functions as IT departments and developers — 100 G	Create a cross functional team to assess ASIS tech. Status: Green
ASIS Infrastructure 4.2	**Backup /BC/DR** (4.21) Take an inventory of the ASIS backup / BC/DR environment — 100 G	**Networks** (4.22) Assess networks for robustness and performance — 100 G	**Applications** (4.23) Assess applications & servers to reduce costs & meet goals — 100 G	**Storage** (4.24) Assess storage and opportunities for virtualisation — 100 G	**Gap Analysis** (4.25) Perform a gap analysis of gaps to fix for transformation — 100 G	Assess existing tools & software to identify gaps & opportunities. Status: Green
Tech Innovation 4.3	**Cloud Based Service** (4.31) Evaluate cloud as an enabler of speed, agility & resiliency — 100 G	**Machine Learning** (4.32) Assess the use of AI machine learning or for improved services — 100 G	**Cybersecurity** (4.33) Make cybersecurity part of DNA with use of DevSecOps — 100 G	**Automation** (4.34) The use of RPA and other technologies to automate processes — 100 G	**AI Governance** (4.35) Build AI governance ethics into products for staff accountability — 100 G	Assess new tech for TOBE infrastructure to aid transformation. Status: Green
Tech Application 4.4	**Business Design** (4.41) Review every element of the business model that affects the consumer experience — 100 G	**Transformation** (4.42) Map the "TOBE" customer journey to business capabilities & value add activities — 100 G	**TOBE Infrastructure** (4.43) Design the "TOBE" infrastructure to deliver the business goals & capabilities — 100 G	**Technology Projects** (4.44) Develop projects based on business requirements to deliver the capabilities — 100 G	**Implementation** (4.45) Use an agile process to implement tech to support new business processes and goals — 100 G	Implement new TOBE infrastructure to support strategy goals & improved CX. Status: Green
Technology Metrics 4.5	**IT Metrics Alignment** (4.51) Align IT metrics with business goals & stakeholders — 100 G	**Uptime** (4.52) The amount of time that systems are available & functional — 100 G	**MTTR Metrics** (4.53) The mean time resolve, respond, repair, or recovery — 100 G	**Customers Satisfied** (4.54) Understand business & customers & improve experience — 100 G	**IT Metrics Reports** (4.55) IT metrics show the value of IT to the rest of the organization — 100 G	Measure success of new technologies for transformation. Status: Green

Status Labels: Workstream No. | % complete | One red, then status red, One orange, then status orange, All green = Complete

4.0 Technology Workstream Plan

Business Transformation: 4.0 Technology						Program Mgr.	Project Mgr.
Goal: Implement new TOBE infrastructure to support strategy goals & improved CX						B. Sykes	P. Giles
						Completion	Overall Status
						15th Feb 2024	Green
Technology Team	**Business Arch.** Overseas design and execution of blueprint for the transformation	**Enterprise Arch.** EA oversee the design of IT orientated enterprise architecture	**Business Part.** Business SMEs and leaders who have inputs & influence	**3rd Party Partners** Most firms require additional specialist skills and experience	**Other Functions** Other functions as IT departments and developers	Create a cross functional team to assess ASIS tech	
4.1	4.11 100 G	4.12 100 G	4.13 100 G	4.14 100 G	4.15 100 G	Status	Green
ASIS Infrastructure	**Backup /BC/DR** Take an inventory of the ASIS backup / BC/ DR environment	**Networks** Assess networks for robustness and performance	**Applications** Assess applications & servers to reduce costs & meet goals	**Storage** Assess storage and opportunities for virtualisation	**Gap Analysis** Perform a gap analysis of gaps to fix for transformation	Assess existing tools & software to identify gaps &opportunities	
4.2	4.21 100 G	4.22 100 G	4.23 100 G	4.24 100 G	4.25 100 G	Status	Green
Tech Innovation	**Cloud Services** Evaluate cloud as an enabler of speed, agility &resiliency	**Machine Learning** Assess the use of AI machine learning or for improved services	**Cybersecurity** Make cybersecurity part of DNA with use of DevSecOps	**Automation** The use of RPA and other technologies to automate processes	**AI Governance** Build AI governance ethics into products for staff accountability	Assess new tech for TOBE infrastructure to aid transformation	
4.3	4.31 100 G	4.32 100 G	4.33 100 G	4.34 100 G	4.35 100 G	Status	Green
Tech Application	**Business Design** Review every element of the business model that affects the consumer experience	**Transformation** Map the "TOBE" customer journey to business capabilities & value add activities	**TOBE Technology** Design the "TOBE" infrastructure to deliver the business goals & capabilities	**Tech. Projects** Develop projects based on business requirements to deliver the capabilities	**Implementation** Use an agile process to implement tech to support new business processes and goals	Implement new TOBE infrastructure to support strategy goals & improved CX	
4.4	4.41 100 G	4.42 100 G	4.43 100 G	4.44 100 G	4.45 100 G	Status	Green
Technology Metrics	**Aligned IT Metrics** Align IT metrics with business goals & stakeholders	**Uptime** The amount of time that systems are available & functional	**MTTR Metrics** The mean time resolve, respond, repair, or recovery	**Customers** Understand business & customers & improve experience	**IT Metrics** IT metrics show the value of IT to the rest of the organization	Measure success of new technologies for transformation	
4.5	4.51 100 G	4.52 100 G	4.53 100 G	4.54 100 G	4.55 100 G	Status	Green
Status Labels	Workstream No.	% complete	One red, then status red, One orange, then status orange, All green = Complete				

4.1 Technology Team

In a technology team working on a business transformation project, there are a few key roles that are important to consider:

- A project manager whom is responsible for the overall planning execution, and delivery of the technology project.
- A business architect is a professional who is responsible for designing the structure and operation of an organization, with a focus on the alignment of business activities with the organization's overall strategy and goals. The role of the business architect is to understand the business as a whole and to design and implement solutions that will enable the organization to achieve its desired outcomes.
- An enterprise architect is responsible for designing and guiding the overall direction of an organization's technology and systems.
- Developers whom are responsible for building and testing the technical solution.
- Quality assurance (QA) engineers whom are responsible for testing the technical solution to ensure it meets the required quality standards.
- A business analyst whom is responsible for understanding the business requirements and translating them into technical solutions.
- A solution architect whom is responsible for designing the overall technical solution and ensuring it meets the business requirements.

Other roles that may be involved in a technology team include business architects, enterprise architects, data engineers, security experts, and DevOps engineers.

The specific roles and responsibilities will depend on the nature of the business transformation project and the technology being used.

4.1 Technology team workstream activities

Business architects	Overseas design and execution of blueprint for the transformation.
Enterprise architects	Enterprise architects oversee the design of IT orientated enterprise architecture.
Business partners	Business SMEs and leaders who have inputs & influence.
Third party partners	Most firms require additional specialist skills and experience.
Other stakeholders	Other functions as IT departments and developers.
Technology team output	Create a cross functional team to assess ASIS technology.

4.1 Technology team questions

Business goals	**What are the business's goals for this transformation?**
	Understanding the transformation objectives is critical for the tech team to be able to align and make the most impact.
Business challenges	**What are the key business challenges and constraints?**
	Identifying and understanding the challenges and constraints that the business is facing can help the technology team to prioritize their efforts and identify the most effective solutions.
Current technologies	**What technologies and systems are currently in place, and how can they be leveraged or improved upon?**
	The technology team will need to understand the current technology landscape in order to identify opportunities to optimize and improve upon existing systems.
Risks and impacts	**What are the potential risks and impacts of the transformation on the business?**
	It is important for the technology team to consider the potential risks and impacts of the transformation on the business, and to develop strategies to mitigate or manage these risks.
Transformation management	**How will the transformation be implemented and managed?**
	The technology team will need to work with the business to develop a plan for implementing and managing the transformation, including identifying the resources and budget needed to support it.

4.1 Technology team plan

General overview	A technology plan for a business transformation should outline the steps that the technology team will take to support the overall business transformation effort. This may include identifying and implementing new technologies, migrating to new systems, integrating different business processes and systems, and training employees on new technologies.
Business goals	Identify the business goals and objectives of the transformation effort.
ASIS assessment	Assess the current technology infrastructure and identify any gaps or weaknesses that need to be addressed in order to support the transformation.
Roadmap	Develop a roadmap for implementing new technologies and systems, including timelines, budgets, and resources required.
Stakeholder engagement	Engage with stakeholders and business leaders to understand their needs and ensure that the technology plan aligns with the overall business transformation strategy.
Training plan	Develop a training plan to ensure that employees are equipped to use the new technologies and systems effectively.
Communications	Communicate the technology plan to the relevant teams and stakeholders, and provide ongoing support and guidance as the transformation progresses.
Continuous monitoring	Continuously monitor and evaluate the effectiveness of the technology plan and make adjustments as needed to ensure the successful completion of the business transformation.

4.1 Technology team best practices

Business problem	Clearly define the business problem or opportunity that the technology is intended to address.
Key stakeholders	Identify key stakeholders and involve them in the planning process to ensure buy-in and support.
Detailed plan	Develop a comprehensive implementation plan that includes all necessary resources, budget, timeline, and milestones.
Technology integration	Ensure that the technology is properly integrated with other systems and processes within the organization.
Training & support	Provide ongoing training and support to ensure that all employees are able to effectively use the technology.
Monitor performance	Monitor the technology's performance and make adjustments as necessary to ensure its ongoing success.
Ongoing comms	Continuously communicate with stakeholders about the progress and value of the technology.

4.1 Technology team risks

General overview	Overall, it is important for the technology team to carefully plan and manage the transformation project in order to mitigate these risks as much as possible.
Lack of resources	There may not be sufficient resources (e.g., budget, personnel, time) to complete the transformation as planned.
Inadequate skills & experience	The team may not have the necessary skills or experience to implement the new technologies or processes required for the transformation.
Integration issues	If the transformation involves the integration of multiple systems or technologies, there may be issues with compatibility or interoperability.
Data migration	Migrating data from legacy systems to new systems can be a complex and time-consuming process, and there is always the risk of data loss or corruption.
Resistance to change	There may be resistance to the transformation from stakeholders within the organization, which can make it difficult to secure the necessary support and resources to complete the project.
Security risks	The introduction of new technologies or processes may introduce security risks that need to be managed.

4.1 Technology team risks

Scope creep	It is important for the technology team to clearly define the scope of the project and ensure that it does not expand beyond the original scope, which can lead to delays and cost overruns. It is important to clearly define the scope of the project and stick to it, as adding additional features or requirements can significantly increase the complexity and risk of the project. This can easily happen being overawed by the technology and forgetting the business goals.
Dependencies	There may be dependencies on other teams or systems that are outside of the control of the technology team. It is important to identify and manage these dependencies effectively to avoid delays or other issues.
Budget & timeline	The project may have tight budget and timeline constraints, which can increase the risk of cost overruns or missed deadlines. It is important to carefully plan and manage the project to stay within budget and meet deadlines.
Change management	A business transformation project can involve significant changes to processes, systems, and organizational structure. It is important to manage and communicate these changes effectively to minimize disruption and ensure the success of the project.

4.1 Technology team lessons learned

Communication & collaboration	The importance of clear communication and collaboration: Business transformations often require significant coordination and communication between different teams and stakeholders. Technology teams can learn the importance of clear communication and collaboration in order to effectively support the transformation.
Risk management	Risk management is important to identify and manage risks throughout the project, including technical risks, project management risks, and business risks. It is important for the technology team to identify and manage risks throughout the transformation process. This may include developing contingency plans in case something goes wrong.
Continuous learning	A business transformation project is an opportunity to learn and improve processes, technologies, and organizational structure. It is important to actively seek out and incorporate lessons learned throughout the project.
Time management	Business transformations can take a significant amount of time, and it is important for the technology team to manage their time effectively and ensure that deadlines are met.
Resource management	It is important for the technology team to manage their resources effectively, including budget, personnel, and equipment, in order to ensure the success of the business transformation.

4.1 Technology team lessons learned

The value of agile	Business transformations often involve a high degree of uncertainty and the need for flexibility. Technology teams can learn the value of agile methodologies, such as sprint planning and continuous delivery, in order to quickly respond to changing needs and priorities.
Data driven decision making	Technology teams can learn the importance of using data to inform decision making during a business transformation. This can involve collecting and analysing data on key performance indicators (KPIs) and using data visualization tools to understand trends and patterns.
Project management	Business transformations often involve complex projects that require strong project management skills. Technology teams can learn the importance of effective project planning, risk management, and resource allocation in order to successfully deliver on the goals of the transformation.
Technology as a business enabler	Technology teams can learn how to use technology as a strategic enabler in order to support the business goals of the transformation. This may involve identifying and implementing new technologies that can help the business operate more efficiently or effectively.

4.2 ASIS Infrastructure

The goal of assessing the current infrastructure for a business transformation program is to determine the current state of the organization's technology and systems, and to identify any areas that may need to be improved or updated in order to support the goals of the business transformation program. This assessment can help organizations understand what resources they have available to support the transformation, and can also help identify any potential constraints or bottlenecks that may need to be addressed in order to ensure the success of the program. Ultimately, the goal is to ensure that the organization's infrastructure is capable of supporting the changes and improvements that will be made as part of the business transformation program.

There are several key components to consider when assessing the current infrastructure for a business transformation program

These include:

- The staff, stakeholders, and customers, will be affected by the transformation program.
- The processes and systems currently in place within the organization will need to be reviewed to identify areas for improvement and to ensure that they are aligned with the goals of the transformation program.
- The data and information currently being used by the organization will need to be analysed to ensure that it is accurate, up-to-date, and relevant to the transformation program.
- The technology and tools being used by the organization should be reviewed to ensure that they are appropriate for the transformation program and that they are being used effectively.
- The governance structures and decision-making processes within the organization should be reviewed to ensure that they are aligned with the goals of the transformation program and that they support the necessary changes.

4.2 ASIS infrastructure workstream activities

Backup /BC/DR	Take an inventory of the ASIS backup / BC/ DR environment.
Networks	Assess networks for robustness and performance.
Applications	Assess applications & servers to reduce costs & meet goals.
Storage	Assess storage and opportunities for virtualisation.
Security	Assess security and data protection.
ASIS infrastructure outcome	Assess existing tools & software to identify gaps & opportunities.

4.2 ASIS infrastructure questions

Pain points	What are the current pain points or challenges that the business is facing with its current infrastructure?
Core business processes	What are the key business processes that are supported by the current infrastructure, and how well are they working?
Current capacity	What is the current capacity of the infrastructure to handle the needs of the business? Is it scalable to support growth?
Reliability	How reliable is the current infrastructure, and how well does it recover from failures or outages?
Security	What is the level of security and data protection provided by the current infrastructure, and how well does it comply with relevant regulations and standards?
Level of integration	What is the level of integration and interoperability between different components of the current infrastructure?
Level of automation	What is the level of automation and ease of use of the current infrastructure, and how well it supports the business needs?
Maintenance and support	What is the current level of maintenance and support for the infrastructure, and how well it supports the business needs?
Infrastructure costs	What is the current cost of the infrastructure, and how does it compare to alternative options?
Future business plans	What are the long-term plans for the business, and how well does the current infrastructure align with those plans?

4.2 ASIS infrastructure plan components

General overview	ASIS (As-Is) analysis is a process of evaluating the current state of an organization's information technology (IT) infrastructure. It involves identifying and documenting the existing IT systems, processes, and resources, and assessing their effectiveness in meeting the organization's current and future needs. By conducting an ASIS analysis of the IT infrastructure, organizations can identify areas for improvement and develop a roadmap for transforming their IT systems to better support their business objectives.
IT strategy	This includes the organization's overall vision and goals for its IT infrastructure, as well as the strategies and plans in place to achieve those goals.
IT architecture	This includes the design of the organization's IT systems, including hardware, software, and networks.
IT processes	This includes the processes and procedures used to manage, maintain, and support the organization's IT infrastructure.
IT resources	This includes the people, skills, and technologies required to support the organization's IT infrastructure.
IT governance	This includes the policies, standards, and controls in place to ensure the effective and efficient use of the organization's IT resources.
IT performance	This includes metrics and measurements used to evaluate the effectiveness and efficiency of the organization's IT systems and processes.

4.2 ASIS infrastructure best practices

Business goals	Start by understanding the business goals and objectives of the transformation program. This will help you determine the infrastructure requirements needed to support these goals.
Gap analysis	Identify any existing gaps or weaknesses in the current infrastructure that may impact the success of the transformation program.
Stakeholder engagement	Engage key stakeholders to gather their input and perspectives on the current infrastructure and how it may need to change to support the transformation program.
Thorough assessment	Conduct a thorough assessment of the current infrastructure, including hardware, software, networks, data storage, and security.
Plan to address gaps	Develop a plan to address any gaps or weaknesses identified in the assessment. This may involve updating or replacing existing infrastructure, or implementing new systems and technologies.
Cost benefit analysis	Consider the costs and benefits of different infrastructure options, and choose the approach that will best support the goals of the transformation program.
Testing & validation of changes	Be sure to test and validate any changes to the infrastructure before implementing them, to ensure that they are reliable and will meet the needs of the business.

4.2 ASIS infrastructure risks

General overview	An AS-IS analysis is a review of the current state of an organization's IT infrastructure. It involves looking at the systems, processes, and technologies that are currently in place and identifying any weaknesses or inefficiencies.
Alignment with business goals	It is important to ensure that the current infrastructure is aligned with the overall goals of the business transformation program. If there is a misalignment, it can lead to problems with the program implementation and hinder its success.
Infrastructure complexity	A complex infrastructure can make it difficult to assess and can increase the risk of issues arising during the transformation process. It is important to really understand the current infrastructure to identify any potential risks.
Legacy systems	If the current infrastructure relies heavily on legacy systems, it may be more difficult and riskier to make changes. It is important to carefully consider the dependencies on these systems and plan for any necessary updates.
Time and cost	Conducting an AS-IS analysis can be time-consuming and costly, as it involves a detailed review of the organization's IT infrastructure.
Disruption to business operations	The process of conducting an AS-IS analysis may disrupt business operations, as staff may need to devote time and resources to the analysis rather than their regular tasks.
Risk of data loss	There is a risk of data loss or breach during the AS-IS analysis, particularly if the organization's IT infrastructure is not properly secured.

4.2 ASIS infrastructure lessons learned

Bottlenecks	Identifying any bottlenecks or inefficiencies in the current infrastructure that could hinder the transformation.
Current limitations	Determining the current capabilities and limitations of the IT infrastructure, and identifying any gaps that need to be addressed in order to support the transformation.
Legacy systems	Identifying any legacy systems or outdated technologies that may need to be replaced or modernized in order to support the transformation.
Security vulnerabilities	Identifying any security vulnerabilities or compliance issues that need to be addressed in order to ensure the IT infrastructure is secure and compliant.
Current IT resources	Assessing the current level of IT staffing and resources, and determining if additional resources or expertise will be needed to support the transformation.
Thorough planning	A key lesson learned is the importance of a thorough assessment of the current infrastructure is crucial to the success of the business transformation program. It allows for the identification of potential risks and issues, and allows for the development of a plan to mitigate those risks.
Stakeholder buy in	It is important to involve key stakeholders in the assessment process to ensure that their needs &concerns are considered. This can help to build buy-in and support for the program.
Ongoing communications	Maintaining ongoing communication with all relevant parties throughout the assessment process can help to ensure that everyone is on the same page and can help to identify any potential issues early on.

4.3 Tech innovation

Technology innovation and disruption can have a significant impact on business transformation programs, as new technologies can enable companies to fundamentally change the way they operate and interact with customers. For example, the widespread adoption of the internet and mobile devices has allowed companies to shift towards online sales and customer service, which has changed the way they do business and the way they interact with their customers. Similarly, the emergence of new technologies such as artificial intelligence and machine learning has the potential to transform a wide range of industries, from healthcare and finance to manufacturing and transportation.

Business transformation programs that are able to effectively incorporate new technologies and take advantage of technological disruption can gain a competitive advantage and drive growth.

However, these programs can also be challenging to implement, as they often require companies to make significant changes to their operations and processes, and they can be difficult to manage. Therefore, it is important for companies to carefully consider how they can incorporate new technologies into their business transformation programs in a way that is manageable and maximizes the potential benefits.

There are many types of technology innovation and disruption that can have an impact on business transformation programs. Some examples include:

- Cloud computing:
- Mobile technologies
- Artificial intelligence
- Machine learning
- Internet of Things (IoT)
- Robotics and automation
- Blockchain
- Virtual and augmented reality

These technologies are being used in a variety of applications, including training, product design, and customer experience.

4.3 Tech innovation workstream activities

Cloud based services	Evaluate cloud as an enabler of speed, agility &resiliency.
Artificial intelligence	Assess the use of AI and machine learning or for improved services.
Cybersecurity	Make cybersecurity part of DNA with use of DevSecOps.
Automation	The use of RPA and other technologies to automate processes.
AI governance	Build AI governance ethics into products for staff accountability.
Tech innovation outcome	Assess new tech for TOBE infrastructure to aid transformation.

4.3 Tech innovation questions

Business problem	What problem is the technology trying to solve, and how will it benefit the business?
Current state of tech	What is the current state of the technology, and how mature is it?
Potential market	What is the potential market for the technology, and how will the business be able to capture a share of that market?
Strategy alignment	How will the technology fit into the overall business strategy and goals?
Risks and challenges	What are the potential risks and challenges associated with implementing the technology, and how will the business mitigate those risks?
Resource availability and requirements	What resources (financial, human, technological) will be required to implement and support the technology?
Integration	How will the technology be integrated into the existing business processes and systems?
Technology timeline	What is the timeline for implementing and scaling the technology?
Success measures	How will the business measure the success of the technology implementation?

4.3 Tech innovation questions

What are the emerging technologies to consider for a business transformation?	
General overview	There are many emerging technologies that businesses may consider when looking to transform their operations. It's important to note that no single technology will be a panacea for all businesses, and the specific technologies that a business should consider will depend on its needs and goals.
Artificial Intelligence	Artificial intelligence (AI) and machine learning are technologies that can be used to automate a wide range of business processes, such as data analysis, customer service, and decision-making.
Internet of things (IOT)	IoT refers to the growing network of connected devices that can collect and exchange data. Businesses can use IoT to improve efficiency, gather data, and gain insights.
Blockchain	This technology allows for secure and transparent record-keeping, and has the potential to disrupt a number of industries.
Virtual & augmented reality	These technologies can be used to create immersive experiences for customers, as well as to train employees and design products.
Robotics	Robotics can be used to automate physical tasks, improving efficiency and potentially reducing the need for human labour.

4.3 Tech innovation plan components

Objectives	Clearly define the goals and objectives of the investigation. This could include identifying new technologies that could improve business processes, increase efficiency, or give the company a competitive edge.
Scope	Define the scope of the investigation, including the specific technologies that will be evaluated and the areas of the business that will be impacted by the technology.
Research and evaluation	Conduct research to identify and evaluate potential technologies. This could include market analysis, competitive analysis, and pilot tests of the technology.
Implementation plan	Develop a detailed plan for implementing the new technology, including budget, timeline, and resources required.
Communication plan	Develop a plan for communicating the results of the investigation and the implementation plan to stakeholders, including employees, customers, and investors.
Risk assessment	Identify and assess any potential risks associated with the implementation of the new technology.
Monitoring and evaluation	Establish a process for ongoing monitoring and evaluation of the technology to ensure it is meeting the goals and objectives of the business.

4.3 Tech innovation best practices

Transformation goals	Clearly define what you hope to achieve through the transformation program, including any specific goals related to technology innovation and disruption. This will help you focus your efforts and assess progress over time.
Key stakeholders	Identify the key stakeholders who will be impacted by the transformation program, including staff, customers, and partners. Engaging these stakeholders early on will help ensure that the program aligns with their needs and issues.
ASIS assessment	Conduct a thorough analysis of your current technology landscape. This should include an assessment of your current technology infrastructure, as well as an analysis of emerging technologies that could impact your business.
Pilot opportunities	Look for opportunities to pilot new technologies. Consider piloting new technologies on a small scale before committing to a full rollout. This will help to test the feasibility and value of the technology, & identify any potential challenges or issues.
Industry trends	Monitor industry trends and competitors. Keep an eye on industry trends and developments, and consider how they might impact your business. It's also important to monitor the technology strategies of your competitors to ensure that you are staying ahead of the curve
Review progress	Measure progress and adjust as needed. Regularly track progress and assess the impact of your technology innovation and disruption efforts. If you find that certain technologies are not delivering the expected results, be willing to pivot and try something else.

4.3 Tech innovation risks

Staying current with technology	One risk is that the technology you adopt may become obsolete quickly, which can be costly if you have to replace it. To mitigate this risk, it's important to stay current with technology trends and do regular assessments to ensure that your technology stack remains relevant.
Compatibility with existing systems	Another risk is that new technology may not be compatible with your existing systems, which can disrupt your operations and potentially cause delays or other issues. To mitigate this risk, it's important to thoroughly test new technology to ensure that it integrates smoothly with your existing systems.
Managing change	Introducing new technology can also be disruptive to your organization and its employees. To minimize this risk, it's important to manage change effectively and provide training and support to ensure that employees are comfortable using the new technology.
Balancing innovation and risk	It's important to carefully weigh the potential benefits of new technology against the potential risks to your organization. This requires a clear understanding of your business objectives and the ability to assess the potential impact of new technology on your operations.
Data protection	As you adopt new technology, it's important to ensure that your data and intellectual property are protected. This may require implementing appropriate security measures and regularly reviewing and updating them.

4.3 Tech innovation lessons learned

A clear business case	Before implementing any new technology, it's important to understand the specific problem or opportunity it is intended to solve. This will help ensure that the technology is aligned with business objectives and provide a clear basis for measuring success.
A thorough assessment	It's essential to carefully assess the potential impact of emerging technologies on all aspects of the business, including operations, organizational structure, and customer experience. This will help identify any potential challenges or risks and allow the business to develop a plan to mitigate them.
A culture of innovation	Business transformation often requires a shift in organizational culture and mindset. Encouraging a culture of innovation and experimentation can help create a more agile and adaptable organization that is better equipped to take advantage of new technologies.
Foster collaboration	Emerging technologies often require collaboration across departments and functional areas. It's important to establish clear lines of communication and encourage teamwork to ensure that everyone is working towards a common goal.

4.4 Tech application

There are several key aspects to consider when implementing technology as part of a business transformation. it is important to ensure that the technology being implemented is aligned with the overall goals and objectives of the business. Also, implementing new technology often requires significant changes to processes, roles, and responsibilities within an organization. It is important to have a plan in place to manage and communicate these changes effectively.

When adopting new technology often requires training for employees to learn how to use it effectively. It is important to provide sufficient training and ongoing support to ensure successful adoption.

A key challenge with new technology is that it can be integrated with existing systems, it is important to ensure a smooth and seamless integration.

Data security is always a high priority, when implementing new technology, as it is important to consider the security of the data being collected, stored, and processed.

With all technology investments, it is important to conduct a cost-benefit analysis to determine the potential return on investment of the new technology and to ensure that it is a viable investment for the business.

4.4 Tech application workstream activities

Business design	Review every element of the business model that affects the consumer experience.
Transformation	Map the "TOBE" customer journey to business capabilities & value add activities.
TOBE infrastructure	Design the "TOBE" infrastructure to deliver the business goals & capabilities.
Technology projects	Develop projects based on business requirements to deliver the capabilities.
Implementation	Use an agile process to implement tech to support new business processes and goals.
Tech application outcome	Implement new TOBE infrastructure to support strategy goals & improved CX.

4.4 Tech application questions

Aligned with goals	How does the new technology support the overall goals and objectives of the business, and how does it align with the customer experience strategy?
Customer experience improvement	How will the new technology improve the customer experience, and what specific customer pain points or needs does it address?
Integration with existing systems	How will the new technology integrate with existing systems and processes, and what impact will it have on the current customer experience?
Training and support	What training and support will be needed for employees to effectively use the new technology, and how will this be provided?
Test and rollout	How will the new technology be tested and rolled out to customers, and what measures will be in place to ensure a smooth transition?
New technology support	How will the new technology be maintained and supported over time, and what measures will be in place to ensure that it continues to deliver a positive customer experience?
Data security	How will the new technology be secured to protect customer data, and what measures will be in place to ensure compliance with relevant regulations?
Potential ROI	What is the potential return on investment of the new technology, and how will its effectiveness be measured and tracked over time

4.4 Tech application plan components

Goals & objectives	Clearly defined goals and objectives help to ensure that the technology is being implemented with a specific purpose in mind, and progress can be measured against these targets.
Stakeholder analysis	Identifying key stakeholders and understanding their needs, concerns, and expectations can help to ensure that the technology implementation is successful and well-received.
Resource assessment	An assessment of the resources required for the technology implementation, including personnel, budget, and infrastructure, will help to ensure that the necessary resources are in place to support the project.
Implementation timeline	A timeline for the implementation will help to ensure that the project stays on track and that key milestones are met.
Communication plan	A communication plan will help to ensure that all stakeholders are kept informed about the progress of the technology implementation, and that any concerns or issues are addressed in a timely manner.
Training plan	A training plan will help to ensure that personnel are able to effectively use the new technology and that it is integrated into their workflows seamlessly.
Support plan	A support plan will ensure that personnel have access to the resources and assistance they need to effectively use the new technology and troubleshoot any issues that may arise.
Risk assessment	A risk assessment will help to identify potential issues that may arise during the technology implementation, and a risk management plan will help to mitigate these risks and ensure the smooth deployment of the technology.

4.4 Tech application best practices

CX goals & objectives	Clearly define what you want to achieve with your technology implementation. Do you want to improve customer satisfaction, increase customer loyalty, or reduce operational costs? Having clear goals will help you choose the right technology and measure the success of your implementation.
Understand customers	Use customer data and feedback to understand their needs and preferences. This will help you choose the right technology and ensure that it addresses the pain points and improves the overall customer experience.
Right technology	Select technology that is reliable, scalable, and user-friendly. Also it needs to integrate with existing systems & processes.
Staff involvement	Your employees will be the ones using the technology, so it is important to involve them in the selection and implementation process. This ensures that they are comfortable using the technology & can provide inputs on how to optimize its use.
Test and refine	Roll out the technology in a pilot program and gather feedback from both customers and employees. Use this feedback to fine-tune the technology and ensure that it is meeting your CX goals.
Train staff	Proper training is essential to ensure that your employees are able to use the technology effectively. Offer ongoing training and support to help them stay up-to-date on new features.
Measure & optimize	Use CX metrics to measure the success of your technology implementation and identify areas for improvement. Continuously optimize and refine the technology to ensure that it is meeting your CX goals.

4.4 Tech application risks

General overview	It is important for organizations to carefully assess these risks and develop strategies to mitigate them before implementing new technology to improve CX.
Cost	Implementing new technology can be expensive, and there is always the risk that the technology will not deliver the desired return on investment.
Complexity	Technology can be complex and difficult to understand, which can make it difficult for employees to use and for the organization to manage.
Change management	Introducing new technology can require significant changes to how an organization operates, which can be disruptive and may be difficult for employees to adapt to.
Integration	If the new technology does not integrate well with existing systems, it can create additional complexity and may not provide the desired benefits.
Security	The increased reliance on technology can also introduce new security risks, such as the risk of cyberattacks.
Dependency	Becoming too reliant on technology can also create risks, such as the risk of system failures or outages that can negatively impact the customer experience.

4.4 Tech application lessons learned

Know your customer needs	Start with a clear understanding of your customers and their needs. Before implementing any technology, it's important to have a deep understanding of your customers and their needs, preferences, and pain points. This will help ensure that the technology you choose is well-aligned with their expectations and needs.
Choose the right technology	Identify the right technology for your business. There are many different types of technology that can be used to improve CX. It's important to carefully evaluate the options and choose the technology that best meets the needs of your business and your customers.
Training	Don't underestimate the importance of training. Implementing new technology can be a significant change for both customers and employees. It's important to provide thorough training to ensure that everyone is able to use the technology effectively and efficiently.
Customer communications	Let your customers know about the new technology and how it will benefit them. This can help to build trust and reduce any potential frustration or confusion.
Monitor & measure impact	It's important to track the impact of the technology on CX and make adjustments as needed. This will help you ensure that the technology is delivering the desired results and improving the overall customer experience.

4.5 Technology Metrics

There are several aspects of metrics that can be useful for measuring the success of a business transformation initiative that involves technology:

- Adoption: This metric measures the extent to which employees are using the new technology or system. This can be tracked through usage data or surveys.
- Productivity: Technology should ideally improve productivity by automating tasks or making work processes more efficient. You can track this metric by comparing productivity before and after the implementation of the new technology.
- Cost savings: If the technology is intended to reduce costs, you can track the costs associated with the old process and compare them to the costs of the new technology to see if there are any savings.
- **Customer satisfaction:** If the technology is intended to improve the customer experience, you can track customer satisfaction levels before and after the implementation of the new technology to see if there has been an improvement.
- **Employee satisfaction:** Technology can also impact employee satisfaction. You can track this metric through surveys or by measuring employee retention rates before and after the implementation of the new technology.
- **Quality:** If the technology is intended to improve the quality of products or services, you can track this metric by comparing the number of defects or errors before and after the implementation of the new technology.
- **Compliance:** If the technology is being used to ensure compliance with regulations or standards, you can track this metric by monitoring the number of compliance incidents before and after the implementation of the new technology.

4.5 Technology metrics workstream activities

IT metrics alignment	Align IT metrics with business goals & stakeholders.
Uptime	The amount of time that systems are available & functional.
MTTR metrics	The mean time resolve, respond, repair, or recovery.
Customer satisfaction	Understand business & customers & improve experience.
IT metrics reports	IT metrics show the value of IT to the rest of the organization.
Technology metrics outcome	Measure success of new technologies for transformation.

4.5 Technology metrics questions

Transformation goals	**What are the goals of the transformation initiative?**
	Identifying the specific goals of the transformation can help determine which metrics will be most relevant for tracking progress and measuring success.
Key stakeholders	**Who are the stakeholders in the transformation?**
	Different stakeholders may have different priorities and concerns, and selecting metrics that are relevant to the needs and interests of these stakeholders can help ensure buy-in and support for the transformation.
Technology application	**How will the technology be used in the transformation?**
	Understanding the role that technology will play in the transformation can help identify metrics that will be useful for tracking its adoption, usage, and impact.
Data available	**What data is available to support the measurement of these metrics?**
	It's important to ensure that the necessary data is available to support the measurement of any chosen metrics.
The use of metrics	**How will the metrics be used?**
	It's important to consider how the metrics will be used, as this can influence which metrics are selected and how they are reported.

4.5 Technology metrics plan components

Clear definition of goals	A clear definition of the goals and objectives of the business transformation initiative: The metrics plan should be based on the specific goals and objectives that the business transformation initiative is trying to achieve. This will help ensure that the metrics chosen are relevant and useful for tracking progress towards these goals.
List of KPIs	The metrics plan should include a list of key performance indicators (KPIs) that will be used to measure progress towards the goals and objectives of the business transformation initiative. These KPIs should be specific, measurable, attainable, relevant, and time-bound (SMART).
Data collection plan	The metrics plan should include a plan for collecting data on the chosen KPIs. This should include details on how the data will be collected, who will be responsible for collecting it, and how often it will be collected.
Data analysis and reporting plan	The metrics plan should include a plan for analysing and reporting on the data collected. This should include details on how the data will be analysed, who will be responsible for analysing it, and how the results of the analysis will be reported to relevant stakeholders.
A plan to drive decision-making	The metrics plan should include a plan for using the data collected and analysed to drive decision making within the organization. This should include details on how the data will be used to inform strategy, allocate resources, and identify areas for improvement.

4.5 Technology metrics best practices

General overview	There are many metrics that can be used to measure the success of a business transformation initiative, and the best ones will depend on the specific goals of the initiative. It's important to identify the key metrics that are most relevant to your transformation goals and to track and measure them regularly to understand the impact of the transformation.
Return on investment (ROI)	This measures the profitability of the transformation initiative by comparing the benefits to the costs.
Time to value	This measures how quickly initiative delivers business value
Adoption rate	This measures the percentage of employees or customers who are using the new technology or processes introduced as part of the transformation.
User satisfaction	This measures how satisfied users are with the new technology or processes.
Process efficiency	This measures how well the new technology or processes are able to streamline and improve business processes.
Data accuracy	This measures the accuracy and completeness of data being collected and used as part of the transformation.
Risk reduction	This measures how well the transformation initiative is able to reduce risk to the business.

4.5 Technology metrics risks

Misalignment	The metrics chosen may not be aligned with the goals of the initiative, which can lead to tracking the wrong things and making poor decisions.
Lack of context	Metrics don't provide context, so it's important to understand the underlying factors that are driving the numbers.
Data quality	If the data being used to calculate the metrics is of poor quality, then the metrics themselves will be unreliable.
Limited perspective	Metrics can only provide a limited perspective on the progress of an initiative, and other factors may be at play that are not being captured by the metrics.
Overreliance	It's important to not rely solely on metrics to make decisions, as they can be misleading if not interpreted correctly.
Bias	There is a risk of bias in the selection and interpretation of metrics, which can impact their usefulness.

4.5 Technology metrics lessons learned

General overview	There are several key lessons that organizations should consider when it comes to selecting and using metrics to evaluate the success of a technology-driven business transformation initiative
Identify the right metrics	It is important to choose metrics that are directly relevant to the goals of the initiative and that will provide meaningful insights into its progress and impact.
Define clear targets	Setting clear targets for each metric will help to progress is measurable and that success can be accurately assessed.
Regular reviews	Monitoring metrics on a regular basis will help to identify any issues or challenges that need to be addressed in order to ensure the success of the initiative.
Informed decision-making	Metrics should be used to inform decision making and to help guide the direction of the initiative.
Be flexible	It may be necessary to adjust the metrics being used or the targets being pursued as the initiative progresses and new information becomes available.

CHANGE IS INEVITABLE. CHANGE IS CONSTANT.

Benjamin Disraeli

5.0 Governance

Governance is an essential part of any business transformation program. It involves establishing policies, procedures, and decision-making processes to ensure that the program is executed effectively and efficiently.

Some key aspects of governance in a business transformation program include:

- Having clearly defined roles and responsibilities is important t for all stakeholders involved in the program, including executives, project managers, and team members.
- There should be a clear process in place for making decisions and resolving issues that arise during the program. This may involve a steering committee or other designated group of decision-makers.
- There should be a robust risk management process in place to identify, assess, and mitigate risks to the program.
- There should be open and transparent communication throughout the program, with regular updates provided to all stakeholders.
- A system should be in place to monitor progress and report on the program's progress to relevant stakeholders.
- A structured approach to change management is essential to ensure that the changes introduced by the transformation program are effectively implemented and adopted.

Without proper governance, it may be difficult to establish clear goals, roles, and responsibilities for the transformation program. This can lead to confusion and lack of progress. Governance helps to ensure that decisions are made in a transparent and accountable manner. Without it, there may be a lack of clear decision-making processes, leading to poor or uninformed decisions.

Governance helps to hold individuals and teams accountable for their actions. Without it, there may be a lack of accountability, leading to a lack of progress or even failure.

The Transformation Playbook

5.0 Governance Plan Linkages

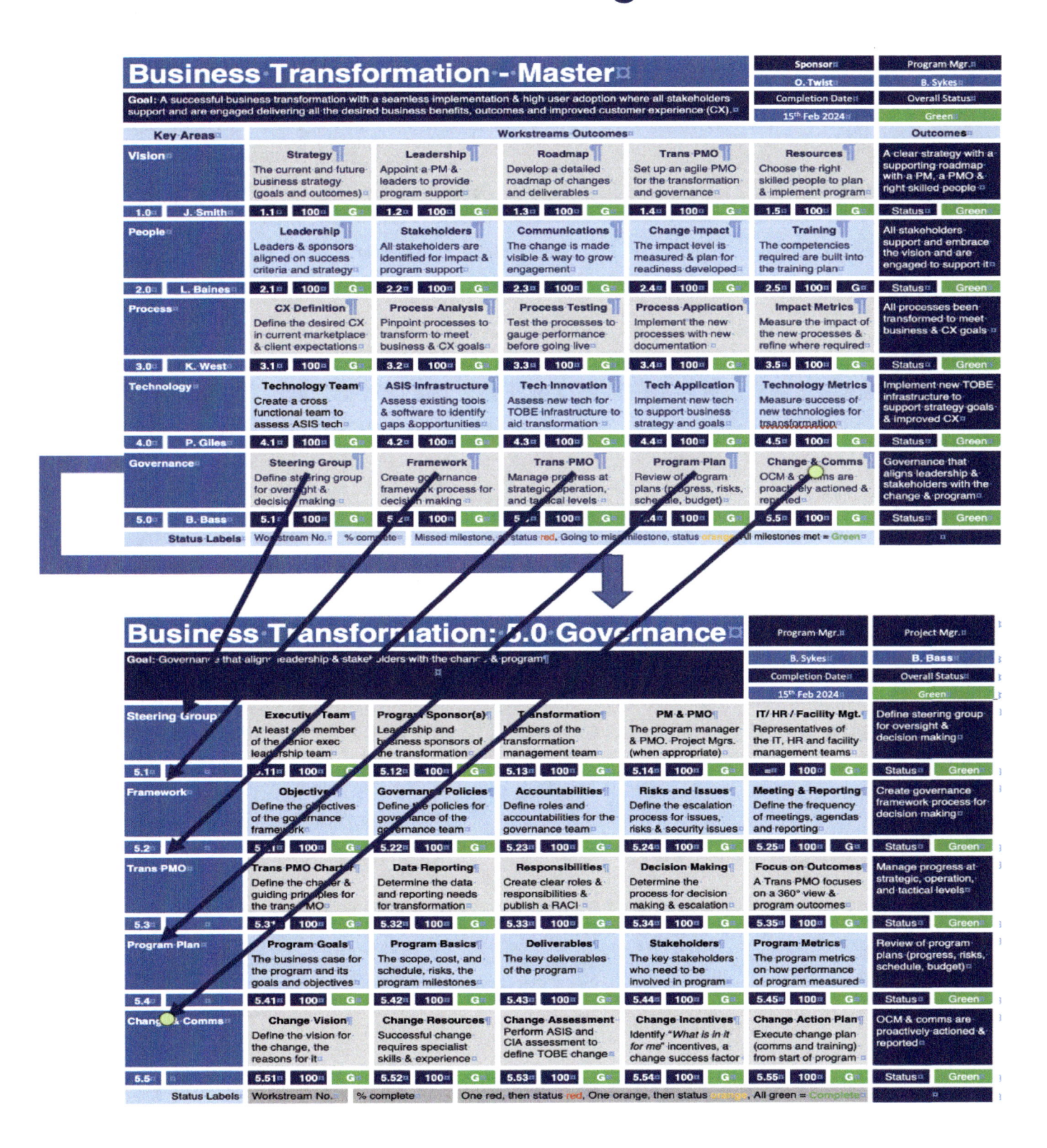

Business Transformation – Master

Sponsor: O. Twist
Program Mgr.: B. Sykes
Completion Date: 15th Feb 2024
Overall Status: Green

Goal: A successful business transformation with a seamless implementation & high user adoption where all stakeholders support and are engaged delivering all the desired business benefits, outcomes and improved customer experience (CX).

Key Areas	Workstreams					Outcomes
Vision 1.0 J. Smith	**Strategy** (1.1) — The current and future business strategy (goals and outcomes) — 100 G	**Leadership** (1.2) — Appoint a PM & leaders to provide program support — 100 G	**Roadmap** (1.3) — Develop a detailed roadmap of changes and deliverables — 100 G	**Trans PMO** (1.4) — Set up an agile PMO for the transformation and governance — 100 G	**Resources** (1.5) — Choose the right skilled people to plan & implement program — 100 G	A clear strategy with a supporting roadmap with a PM, a PMO & right skilled people — Status: Green
People 2.0 L. Baines	**Leadership** (2.1) — Leaders & sponsors aligned on success criteria and strategy — 100 G	**Stakeholders** (2.2) — All stakeholders are identified for impact & program support — 100 G	**Communications** (2.3) — The change is made visible & way to grow engagement — 100 G	**Change Impact** (2.4) — The impact level is measured & plan for readiness developed — 100 G	**Training** (2.5) — The competencies required are built into the training plan — 100 G	All stakeholders support and embrace the vision and are engaged to support it — Status: Green
Process 3.0 K. West	**CX Definition** (3.1) — Define the desired CX in current marketplace & client expectations — 100 G	**Process Analysis** (3.2) — Pinpoint processes to transform to meet business & CX goals — 100 G	**Process Testing** (3.3) — Test the processes to gauge performance before going live — 100 G	**Process Application** (3.4) — Implement the new processes with new documentation — 100 G	**Impact Metrics** (3.5) — Measure the impact of the new processes & refine where required — 100 G	All processes been transformed to meet business & CX goals — Status: Green
Technology 4.0 P. Giles	**Technology Team** (4.1) — Create a cross functional team to assess ASIS tech — 100 G	**ASIS Infrastructure** (4.2) — Assess existing tools & software to identify gaps & opportunities — 100 G	**Tech Innovation** (4.3) — Assess new tech for TOBE infrastructure to aid transformation — 100 G	**Tech Application** (4.4) — Implement new tech to support business strategy and goals — 100 G	**Technology Metrics** (4.5) — Measure success of new technologies for transformation — 100 G	Implement new TOBE infrastructure to support strategy goals & improved CX — Status: Green
Governance 5.0 B. Bass	**Steering Group** (5.1) — Define steering group for oversight & decision making — 100 G	**Framework** (5.2) — Create governance framework process for decision making — 100 G	**Trans PMO** (5.3) — Manage progress at strategic, operation, and tactical levels — 100 G	**Program Plan** (5.4) — Review of program plans (progress, risks, schedule, budget) — 100 G	**Change & Comms** (5.5) — OCM & comms are proactively actioned & reported — 100 G	Governance that aligns leadership & stakeholders with the change & program — Status: Green

Status Labels: Workstream No. | % complete | Missed milestone, status red | Going to miss milestone, status orange | All milestones met = Green

---

Business Transformation: 5.0 Governance

Program Mgr.: B. Sykes
Project Mgr.: B. Bass
Completion Date: 15th Feb 2024
Overall Status: Green

Goal: Governance that aligns leadership & stakeholders with the change & program.

Steering Group 5.1	**Executive Team** (5.11) — At least one member of the senior exec leadership team — 100 G	**Program Sponsor(s)** (5.12) — Leadership and business sponsors of the transformation — 100 G	**Transformation** (5.13) — Members of the transformation management team — 100 G	**PM & PMO** (5.14) — The program manager & PMO. Project Mgrs. (when appropriate) — 100 G	**IT / HR / Facility Mgt.** — Representatives of the IT, HR and facility management teams — 100 G	Define steering group for oversight & decision making — Status: Green
Framework 5.2	**Objectives** (5.21) — Define the objectives of the governance framework — 100 G	**Governance Policies** (5.22) — Define the policies for governance of the governance team — 100 G	**Accountabilities** (5.23) — Define roles and accountabilities for the governance team — 100 G	**Risks and Issues** (5.24) — Define the escalation process for issues, risks & security issues — 100 G	**Meeting & Reporting** (5.25) — Define the frequency of meetings, agendas and reporting — 100 G	Create governance framework process for decision making — Status: Green
Trans PMO 5.3	**Trans PMO Charter** (5.31) — Define the charter & guiding principles for the trans PMO — 100 G	**Data Reporting** (5.32) — Determine the data and reporting needs for transformation — 100 G	**Responsibilities** (5.33) — Create clear roles & responsibilities & publish a RACI — 100 G	**Decision Making** (5.34) — Determine the process for decision making & escalation — 100 G	**Focus on Outcomes** (5.35) — A Trans PMO focuses on a 360° view & program outcomes — 100 G	Manage progress at strategic, operation, and tactical levels — Status: Green
Program Plan 5.4	**Program Goals** (5.41) — The business case for the program and its goals and objectives — 100 G	**Program Basics** (5.42) — The scope, cost, and schedule, risks, the program milestones — 100 G	**Deliverables** (5.43) — The key deliverables of the program — 100 G	**Stakeholders** (5.44) — The key stakeholders who need to be involved in program — 100 G	**Program Metrics** (5.45) — The program metrics on how performance of program measured — 100 G	Review of program plans (progress, risks, schedule, budget) — Status: Green
Change & Comms 5.5	**Change Vision** (5.51) — Define the vision for the change, the reasons for it — 100 G	**Change Resources** (5.52) — Successful change requires specialist skills & experience — 100 G	**Change Assessment** (5.53) — Perform ASIS and CIA assessment to define TOBE change — 100 G	**Change Incentives** (5.54) — Identify "What is in it for me" incentives, a change success factor — 100 G	**Change Action Plan** (5.55) — Execute change plan (comms and training) from start of program — 100 G	OCM & comms are proactively actioned & reported — Status: Green

Status Labels: Workstream No. | % complete | One red, then status red | One orange, then status orange | All green = Complete

5.0 Governance Workstream Plan

Business Transformation: 5.0 Governance						Program Mgr.	Project Mgr.
Goal: Governance that aligns leadership & stakeholders with the change & program						B. Sykes	B. Bass
						Completion	Overall Status
						15th Feb 2024	Green
Steering Group	**Executive Team** — Ensure one member of senior exec team in governance group	**Sponsor(s)** — Identify leaders and business sponsors of the transformation	**Transformation** — Identify members of the transformation management team	**PM & PMO** — The program manager & PMO. Project Mgrs. (when appropriate)	**IT/ HR / Facility** — Representatives of the IT, HR and facility management teams	Define steering group for oversight & decision making	
5.1	5.11 / 100 / G	5.12 / 100 / G	5.13 / 100 / G	5.14 / 100 / G	= / 100 / G	Status	Green
Framework	**Objectives** — Define the objectives of the governance framework	**Governance** — Define the policies for governance of the governance team	**Accountabilities** — Define roles and accountabilities for the governance team	**Risks and Issues** — Define the escalation process for issues, risks & security issues	**Meetings** — Define the frequency of meetings, agendas and reporting	Create governance framework process for decision making	
5.2	5.21 / 100 / G	5.22 / 100 / G	5.23 / 100 / G	5.24 / 100 / G	5.25 / 100 / G	Status	Green
PMO Govern	**PMO Charter** — Define the charter & guiding principles for the trans PMO	**Data Reporting** — Determine the data and reporting needs for transformation	**Responsibilities** — Create clear roles & responsibilities & publish a RACI	**Decision Making** — Determine the process for decision making & escalation	**Outcomes** — A Trans PMO focuses on a 360° view & program outcomes	Manage progress at strategic, operation, and tactical levels	
5.3	5.31 / 100 / G	5.32 / 100 / G	5.33 / 100 / G	5.34 / 100 / G	5.35 / 100 / G	Status	Green
Program Plan	**Program Goals** — Review business case for the program and its objectives	**Program Basics** — Review scope, cost, and schedule, risks, the milestones	**Deliverables** — Review key program deliverables and timeline	**Stakeholders** — Review stakeholders who need to be involved in program	**Program Metrics** — Review program metrics on program performance	Review of program plans (progress, risks, schedule, budget)	
5.4	5.41 / 100 / G	5.42 / 100 / G	5.43 / 100 / G	5.44 / 100 / G	5.45 / 100 / G	Status	Green
Change & Comms	**Change Vision** — Review the vision for change and the reasons for it	**Resources** — Ensure resources with change specialist skills & experience	**Assessment** — Review ASIS and CIA assessment for defined TOBE change	**Change Plans** — Review change plan with appropriate comms and training	**Change Feedback** — Review feedback on acceptance of change and change plan	OCM & comms are proactively actioned & reported	
5.5	5.51 / 100 / G	5.52 / 100 / G	5.53 / 100 / G	5.54 / 100 / G	5.55 / 100 / G	Status	Green

Status Labels | Workstream No. | % complete | One red, then status red, One orange, then status orange, All green = Complete

5.1 Steering Group

A governance steering group is a group of individuals responsible for providing strategic direction and oversight for a business transformation program. The group typically consists of senior leaders from different departments or business units within the organization, and its role is to ensure that the transformation program aligns with the overall goals and objectives of the organization.

The governance steering group is responsible for making key decisions about the direction of the transformation program, including setting priorities, allocating resources, and managing risk. It is also responsible for communicating the progress and results of the program to stakeholders and ensuring that the program is on track to deliver the expected benefits.

A poor governance steering group can have a number of negative impacts on a business transformation program.

First and foremost, it can hinder the progress of the program, as the steering group is responsible for making key decisions and providing direction for the program. If the group is not functioning effectively, it may be unable to make timely decisions or provide clear guidance, which can cause delays and confusion.

Additionally, a poor governance steering group may struggle to effectively communicate and engage with stakeholders, leading to a lack of buy-in and support for the program. This can make it difficult to secure the necessary resources and support needed to successfully implement the changes being proposed. Finally, a poor governance steering group may not be able to effectively manage risks and issues that arise during the transformation program, leading to potential problems or setbacks that could have been avoided with better governance.

5.1 Steering group workstream activities

Executive	Ensure one member of senior exec team in governance group.
Sponsor(s)	Identify leaders and business sponsors of the transformation.
Transformation	Identify members of the transformation management team.
PM & PMO	The program manager & PMO. Project managers. (when appropriate).
IT / HR / Facility	Representatives of the IT, HR and facility management teams.
Steering group outcome	Define steering group for oversight & decision making.

The Transformation Playbook

5.1 Steering group questions

General overview	The key questions asked by a governance steering group for a business transformation program may vary depending on the specific goals and objectives of the program, as well as the needs and concerns of the organization. By answering these types of questions, the governance steering group can help ensure that the business transformation program is well-planned, well-managed, and aligned with the strategic goals of the organization.
Scope and scale of program	What is the scope and scale of the business transformation program?
Program objectives	What are the objectives of the program, and how will they be achieved?
Resource requirements	What resources (financial, human, technological, etc.) will be required to successfully implement the program?
Risks and challenges	What risks and challenges are anticipated, and how will they be managed?
Governance structure	What is the governance structure for the program, and who is responsible for decision-making and oversight?
Progress measures	How will progress be tracked and measured, and how will the success of the program be evaluated?
Timeline	What is the timeline for the program, and what are the key milestones?
Communications	How will the program be communicated to stakeholders, and how will their input be solicited and incorporated?

5.1 Steering group plan components

Objectives	The group should have clear and measurable objectives that align with the overall goals of the transformation program.
Membership	The group should include key stakeholders from different parts of the organization, such as senior leaders, subject matter experts, and employees who will be directly impacted by the transformation.
Decision-making authority	The group should have the authority to make decisions that guide the direction and implementation of the business transformation program.
Communications & collaboration	The group should establish effective channels for communication and collaboration, both within the group and with other stakeholders in the organization.
Risk management	The group should identify and manage potential risks that could impact the success of the transformation program.
Performance management	The group should establish metrics to measure the performance of the business transformation program and report on progress to key stakeholders.

5.1 Steering group best practices

Roles & responsibilities	Establishing clear roles and responsibilities for all members of the steering group. This includes defining the authority of the group and the decision-making process.
Scope & objectives	Clearly defining the scope and objectives of the business transformation program, and the outcomes and benefits.
Representative of all relevant stakeholders	Ensuring that the steering group is representative of all relevant stakeholders in the organization, including business leaders, subject matter experts, and key employees.
Meetings & communications	Establishing regular meetings and communication channels to ensure that the steering group stays informed about the progress of the transformation program and can make informed decisions.
Risks and issues process	Establishing a process for managing risks and addressing issues as they arise, including a mechanism for escalating concerns or issues to the steering group as needed.
Steering group resources	Ensuring that the steering group has the necessary resources, including budget, personnel, and technology, to effectively oversee the transformation program.
Measuring progress	Tracking and measuring progress against the defined objectives and outcomes, and using this information to make adjustments as needed.

5.1 Steering group risks

Lack of buy-in from stakeholders	If key stakeholders do not support the transformation program, it can be difficult to drive change and achieve the desired results.
Resistance to change	Some employees may resist the changes being implemented as part of the transformation program, which can lead to reduced productivity and morale.
Communication breakdown	Miscommunication or lack of communication can lead to misunderstandings and confusion, which can hinder the progress of the transformation program.
Scope creep	The transformation program may evolve and change as it progresses, leading to scope creep and the potential for the program to become unmanageable.
Budget and resource constraints	The transformation program may require significant resources and budget, and if these are not properly managed, it can lead to delays or failure.
Clear goals and objectives	Without clear goals and objectives, it can be difficult to measure the success of the transformation program and identify areas for improvement.

5.1 Steering group lessons learned

Clearly defined roles	Clearly define the roles and responsibilities of the steering group and all other stakeholders, including the project team and executive sponsors.
Clear decision-making processes	Establish clear decision-making processes and communication channels, and ensure that all stakeholders are aware of them.
Realistic expectations	Set realistic expectations and goals for the transformation program, and regularly review and adjust them as needed.
Strong sponsorship	Ensure that there is strong executive sponsorship and support for the transformation program.
Ongoing improvement	Foster a culture of continuous improvement and encourage all stakeholders to share ideas and feedback.
Monitor progress	Monitor progress regularly and adjust course as needed to ensure that the transformation program stays on track.
Good relationships	Maintain good relationships with all stakeholders and communicate openly and transparently throughout the transformation process.
Celebrate success	Take the time to celebrate successes and recognize the contributions of all stakeholders.

5.2 Framework

A governance framework is a set of guidelines, rules, and processes that are used to govern and manage a business transformation program. It defines the roles, responsibilities, and decision-making authority of different stakeholders involved in the program, as well as the processes and procedures that will be followed to ensure that the program is successfully implemented. A governance framework is typically developed at the outset of a business transformation program and is designed to provide a clear and consistent set of rules and guidelines that will guide the program as it progresses. It is an important tool for helping to ensure that the program stays on track, meets its objectives, and delivers the desired outcomes.

Not having a governance framework for a business transformation program can have a number of negative impacts on the organization.

Without a governance framework, it can be difficult to establish clear goals, objectives, and priorities for the transformation program, leading to confusion and uncertainty among stakeholders.

Also, it can be difficult to track progress and measure the success of the transformation program, making it hard to identify potential issues or correct as needed.

Without a clear governance structure in place, it can be difficult to engage and involve key stakeholders in the transformation process, leading to a lack of buy-in and support for the program.

In addition, it can be difficult to identify and manage risks associated with the transformation program, potentially leading to delays, budget overruns, or even failure of the program.

Overall, having a well-defined governance framework in place is critical for ensuring the success of a business transformation program. It helps to provide direction, visibility, and stakeholder engagement, while also helping to mitigate risks and challenges.

5.2 Framework workstream activities

Objectives	Define the objectives of the governance framework.
Governance policies	Define the policies for governance of the governance team.
Accountabilities	Define roles and accountabilities for the governance team.
Risks & issues	Define the escalation process for issues, risks & security issues.
Meetings & reporting	Define the frequency of meetings, agendas and reporting.
Framework outcome	Create governance framework process for decision making.

5.2 Framework questions

Program purpose	What is the purpose of the business transformation program?
Program sponsor	Who is responsible for overseeing the program?
Program structure	How will the program be structured and organized?
Key stakeholders	What are the key stakeholders and how will they be involved in the program?
Decision-making	How will decisions be made and by whom?
Program budget	How will the program be funded and how will the budget be managed?
Progress monitoring	How will progress be monitored and how will success be measured?
Risk management	What risks are associated with the program and how will they be managed?
Communications	How will communication be managed during the program?
Program sustainability	How will the program be sustained after it is completed?

5.2 Framework plan components

Vision and goals	Clearly define the purpose and objectives of the business transformation program.
Stakeholder analysis	Identify the key stakeholders who will be impacted by the program and determine their level of influence and interest.
Governance structure	Define the roles and responsibilities of the individuals or groups that will be responsible for overseeing the program, as well as the decision-making processes that will be used.
Communication plan	Develop a plan for managing communication during the program, including how the information will be shared with stakeholders and how feedback is collected and used.
Risk management plan	Identify and assess the risks associated with the program and develop a plan for how they will be mitigated or managed.
Resource plan	Identify the resources that will be required to successfully implement the program, including budget, personnel, and other resources.
Implementation plan	Outline the steps that will be taken to implement the program, including any milestones or deliverables.
Monitoring & evaluation plan	Develop a plan for how the program will be monitored and evaluated, including how success will be measured.
Sustainability plan	Determine how the benefits of the program will be sustained after it is completed.

5.2 Framework best practices

Clear purpose & objectives	Clearly define the purpose and objectives of the program: It is important to have a clear understanding of the purpose and goals of the business transformation program in order to guide decision-making and ensure that the program is aligned with the overall strategy of the organization.
Early involvement of stakeholders	Involve key stakeholders in the design and implementation of the program: Engaging key stakeholders in the design and implementation of the program can help buy in and support for the program, as well as provide valuable insights.
Clear governance structure	Establish a clear governance structure and decision-making process: Define the roles and responsibilities for those individuals or groups responsible for overseeing the program, as well as the processes used to make decisions.
Detailed comms plan	A robust comms plan is critical for ensuring that stakeholders are informed and engaged throughout the program.
Identify & assess risks	It is important to identify and assess the risks associated with the program and develop a risk management plan.
Monitoring process	Establish a process for monitoring and evaluating the program: Develop a plan for how the program will be monitored and evaluated, including success measures.
Plan for sustainability	Determine how the benefits of the program will be sustained after it is completed.
Review & adjust governance framework	It is important to regularly review and assess the effectiveness of the governance framework and make adjustments as needed to ensure that it is effective in supporting the business transformation program.

5.2 Framework risks

Lack of direction	Without a clear governance framework, it can be difficult stay aligned that it stays aligned with the overall business strategy.
Lack of accountability	In the absence of a governance structure and decision-making process, it can be difficult to hold people accountable for their actions or decisions related to the program.
poor communication	A comprehensive comms plan is required as it can be difficult to effectively share information and solicit feedback from stakeholders, leading to misunderstandings and conflicts.
Increased risk	A process for identifying and managing risks is needed as the program may be more vulnerable to unforeseen events or issues that could disrupt or derail the program.
Inefficient use of resources	There needs to be a resource management plan otherwise there may be an unnecessary duplication of efforts or a lack of coordination, leading to the inefficient use of resources.
Inability to measure success	Without a plan for monitoring and evaluating the program, it may be difficult to determine whether the program is achieving its goals and realize the intended benefits.
Lack of sustainability	Without a plan for sustaining the benefits of the program after it is completed, the impact of the program may be limited and short-lived.

5.2 Framework lessons learned

Improved direction & alignment	A clear governance framework can help to ensure that the program stays aligned with the overall strategy of the organization and that all efforts are focused on achieving the defined goals and objectives.
Enhanced accountability	A well-defined governance structure and decision-making process can help to hold individuals or groups accountable for their actions and decisions related to the program.
Improved communications	A communication plan can help to ensure that stakeholders are informed and engaged throughout the program and that feedback is solicited and incorporated into decision-making.
Enhanced risk management	A process for identifying and managing program risks can help to minimize the impact of unforeseen events or issues.
Efficient use of resources	A clear plan for managing resources can help to ensure that efforts are coordinated and resources are used efficiently.
Improved ability to measure success	A monitoring and evaluation plan can help to determine whether the program is achieving its goals and realize the intended benefits.
Sustained benefits	A sustainability plan can help to ensure that the benefits of the program are sustained after it is completed.

5.3 PMO Govern

A transformation Program Management Office (PMO) is a dedicated team or unit that is responsible for managing and supporting the business transformation program. Here are some key aspects of having a transformation PMO in place:

- A transformation PMO can provide centralized management and oversight of the program, ensuring that all efforts are aligned with the overall goals and objectives of the program.
- The transformation PMO can help to coordinate and align the activities of different teams and functions involved in the program, ensuring that efforts are focused and coordinated.
- The transformation PMO can be responsible for managing and allocating resources for the program, including personnel, budget, and other resources.
- The transformation PMO can manage communication with stakeholders and ensure that feedback is solicited.
- The transformation PMO can identify and assess risks associated with the program and develop a plan for how they will be managed.
- The transformation PMO can develop and implement a plan for monitoring and evaluating the progress of the program and measuring success.
- The transformation PMO can develop and implement a plan for sustaining the benefits of the program after it is completed.

Not having a transformation Program Management Office (PMO) in place for a business transformation program can have several negative impacts:

- Lack of centralized management
- Lack of coordination and alignment
- Inefficient use of resources
- Poor communication and stakeholder engagement
- Increased risk
- Inability to measure success
- Lack of sustainability

5.3 PMO Govern workstream activities

PMO charter	Define the charter & guiding principles for the trans PMO.
Data reporting	Determine the data and reporting needs for transformation.
Responsibilities	Create clear roles & responsibilities & publish a RACI.
Decision-making	Determine the process for decision making & escalation/
Focus on outcomes	A Trans PMO focuses on a 360° view & program outcomes.
PMO Govern outcome	Manage governance and progress at all program levels.

5.3 PMO Govern questions

Program goals	What is the overall goal and objective of the business transformation program?
Key stakeholders	Who are the key stakeholders and how will they be engaged in the program?
Program structure	How will the program be structured and organized?
Program resources	What resources will be required to successfully implement the program, and how will they be managed?
Progress monitoring & success metrics	How will progress be monitored and how will success be measured?
Program risks	What risks are associated with the program and how will they be managed?
Program comms	How will communication be managed during the program?
Program sustainability	How will the program be sustained after it is completed?
Trans PMO staffing	How will the transformation PMO be structured and staffed?
Transformation PMO funding	How will the transformation PMO be funded and how will the budget be managed?

5.3 PMO Govern plan components

Vision and goals	Clearly define the purpose and objectives of the business transformation program and how the PMO will support the achievement of these goals.
Stakeholder analysis	Identify the key stakeholders who will be impacted by the program and determine their level of influence and interest, as well as how the PMO will engage with them.
Governance structure	Define the roles and responsibilities of the PMO and how it will fit within the overall governance structure of the program.
Resource plan	Identify the resources that will be required to support the PMO, including personnel, budget, and other resources, and how they will be managed.
Comms plan	Develop a plan for how communication will be managed during the program, including how information will be shared with stakeholders and how feedback collected and used.
Risk management plan	Identify and assess the risks associated with the program and develop a plan for how they will be mitigated or managed.
Implementation plan	Outline the steps that will be taken to implement the PMO and support the program, including any milestones or deliverables.
Monitoring & evaluation plan	Develop a plan for how the program will be monitored and evaluated, including how success will be measured.
Sustainability plan	Determine how the PMO will be sustained after the program is completed.

5.3 PMO Govern best practices

Clear PMO purpose	Clearly define the purpose and objectives of the PMO as It is important to have a clear understanding of the purpose and goals of the PMO in order to guide decision-making and ensure that it is aligned with the overall program strategy.
Stakeholder involvement	Involve key stakeholders in the design and implementation of the PMO as engaging key stakeholders in the design and implementation of the PMO can help to ensure buy-in and support for the program, as well as provide valuable insights
Clear governance structure	Establish a clear governance structure and decision-making process to define the roles and responsibilities of the PMO and how it will fit within the overall governance structure of the program, as well as the decision-making processes.
Detailed comms plan	A robust comms plan is critical for ensuring that stakeholders are informed and engaged throughout the program and that feedback is solicited and incorporated into decision-making.
Identify & assess risks	It is important to identify and assess the program risks and develop a plan for how they will be managed.
Monitoring & evaluation	Establish a process for monitoring and evaluating the program. Develop a plan for how the program will be monitored and evaluated, including success measures
Sustainability plan	Determine how the PMO will be sustained after the program is completed.
Review PMO	Review and adjust the PMO as needed. It is important to regularly review and assess the effectiveness of the PMO and make adjustments as needed to ensure that it is effective in supporting the business transformation program.

5.3 PMO Govern risks

Lack of direction	Without a clear governance framework in place, it can be difficult to establish a clear direction for the PMO and ensure that it stays aligned with the overall strategy of the program.
Lack of accountability	Without a clear governance structure and decision-making process, it can be difficult to hold the PMO accountable for its actions or decisions related to the program.
Poor communications	Without a comprehensive communication plan, it can be difficult to effectively share information and solicit feedback from stakeholders, leading to misunderstandings and potential conflicts.
Increased risk	Without a process for identifying and managing risks, the program may be more vulnerable to unforeseen events or issues that could disrupt or derail the program.
Inefficient use of resources	Without a clear plan for how resources will be managed, there may be unnecessary duplication of efforts or a lack of coordination, leading to the inefficient use of resources.
Inability to measure success	Without a plan for monitoring and evaluating the program, it may be difficult to determine whether the program is achieving its goals and realize the intended benefits.
Lack of sustainability	Without a plan for sustaining the PMO after the program is completed, the impact of the program may be limited and short-lived.

5.3 PMO Govern lessons learned

Improved direction & alignment	A clear governance framework can help to ensure that the PMO stays aligned with the overall strategy of the program and that all efforts are focused on achieving the defined goals and objectives.
Enhanced accountability	A well-defined governance structure and decision-making process can help to hold the PMO accountable for its actions and decisions related to the program.
Improved comms	A comprehensive communication plan can help to ensure that stakeholders are informed and engaged throughout the program and that feedback is solicited and incorporated into decision-making.
Enhanced risk management	A process for identifying and managing risks can help to minimize the impact of unforeseen events or issues on the program.
Efficient use of resources	A clear plan for managing resources can help to ensure that efforts are coordinated and resources are used efficiently.
Improved ability to measure success	A monitoring and evaluation plan can help to determine whether the program is achieving its goals and realize the intended benefits.
Sustained benefits	A sustainability plan can help to ensure that the benefits of the program are sustained after it is completed.

5.4 Program Plan

There are several key aspects that should be included in a program plan for a business transformation initiative. These may include:

- Clearly define the goals and objectives of the business transformation initiative, including any specific targets or metrics that will be used to measure success.
- Define the scope of the business transformation initiative, including which business processes, systems, and/or organizational units will be affected.
- Identify all of the key stakeholders who will be impacted by the business transformation initiative.
- Identify the specific outcomes that the business transformation initiative will produce.
- Create a timeline for the business transformation initiative, including key milestones and deadlines.
- Establish a budget for the business transformation initiative.
- Identify and assess potential risks that may impact the success of the business transformation initiative, and outline a plan for managing those risks.
- Develop a plan for communicating with stakeholders about the business transformation initiative, including how updates and progress will be shared.
- Identify any training needs that will be required to support the business transformation initiative.

Not having a good program plan for a business transformation initiative can have a number of negative impacts. Without a clear plan, it can be difficult for the team to know what needs to be done and how to do it. This can lead to confusion and a lack of focus, which can be detrimental to the success of the initiative. A well-defined program plan helps to identify and mitigate potential risks and challenges that may arise during the transformation process. Without a plan, the initiative is more likely to encounter unexpected problems that could derail the project.

5.4 Program plan workstream activities

Program goals	Review business case for the program and its objectives.
Program basics	Review scope, cost, and schedule, risks, the milestones.
Deliverables	Review key program deliverables and timeline.
Stakeholders	Review stakeholders who need to be involved in program.
Program metrics	Review program metrics on program performance.
Program plan outcome	Review of program plans (progress, risks, schedule, budget)

5.4 Program plan questions

Overall transformation goal	What is the overall goal of the business transformation initiative?
Specific objectives	What are the specific objectives that need to be achieved in order to reach the overall goal?
Impacted stakeholders	Who are the stakeholders that will be impacted by the business transformation initiative, and how will they be involved in the planning process?
Resource requirements	What resources (e.g. budget, personnel, technology) will be required to successfully implement the business transformation initiative?
Potential risks and challenges	What are the potential risks and challenges associated with the transformation initiative, and how will they be addressed?
Timeline & milestones	What is the timeline for implementing the business transformation initiative, and what are the key milestones that need to be achieved along the way?
Program metrics	How will the success of the business transformation initiative be measured, and the metrics will be used to track progress?
Program comms	How will the business transformation initiative be communicated to all relevant stakeholders, and what support will be provided to ensure its success?

5.4 Program plan components

Clear vision and objectives	The program should have a clear vision of what the transformation is trying to achieve, and specific, measurable, achievable, relevant, and time-bound (SMART) objectives.
Program roadmap	The program should have a roadmap that outlines the key activities, milestones, & dependencies of the transformation.
Governance structure	There should be a clear governance structure in place that defines roles and responsibilities, decision-making processes, and communication channels.
Budget & resource plan	The program should have a budget that covers all the costs associated with the transformation, and a plan for allocating resources (e.g., people, equipment) to the different activities.
Risk management plan	The program should have a plan for identifying, assessing, and managing risks that may arise during the transformation.
Comms plan	There should be a plan for communicating with all stakeholders (e.g., staff, customers, partners) about the transformation, including any changes that may affect them.
Training & development plan	The program should have a plan for training and developing the skills of staff who will be involved in the transformation.
Change management plan	The program should have a plan for managing and supporting staff with the changes from the transformation.
Performance plan	A plan for measuring the performance of the transformation, including KPIs and target levels of performance.
Implementation plan	The program should have a detailed plan for implementing the different activities and deliverables of the transformation.

5.4 Program plan best practices

Define initiative scope	Clearly define the goals and objectives of the initiative, and what will be included and excluded.
Identify stakeholders	Identify all the stakeholders who will be impacted by the initiative and involve them in the planning process.
Develop a roadmap	Create a roadmap that outlines the key steps and milestones of the initiative.
Create a budget	Establish a budget for the initiative, including any resources or investments that will be required.
Assign roles & responsibilities	Clearly define the roles and responsibilities of all team members involved in the initiative.
Identify risks & challenges	Identify any potential risks or challenges that could impact the success of the initiative and develop contingency plans.
Communicate the plan	Communicate the program plan to all relevant stakeholders, including team members, leadership, and any external partners or vendors.
Monitor & adjust	Regularly monitor the progress of the initiative and make adjustments as needed to ensure its success.

5.4 Program plan risks

Cost overruns	If the program plan is not well-defined and lacks clear objectives, it can be difficult to accurately estimate the costs of the initiative. This can lead to cost overruns, which can negatively impact the financial health of the organization.
Schedule delays	A poorly-planned program can also suffer from schedule delays, which can disrupt business operations and hinder the organization's ability to achieve its goals.
Reduced quality	A rushed or poorly-planned initiative may result in a lower-quality product or service, which can lead to customer dissatisfaction and negative impacts on the firm's reputation.
Reduced adoption	If the business transformation initiative is not well-communicated or well-received by employees, it may be difficult to achieve widespread adoption and realize the full benefits of the program.
Missed opportunities	A poorly-planned initiative may fail to address key business needs or opportunities, leading to missed opportunities for growth and innovation.
Increased risk	A rushed or poorly-planned initiative can also increase the risk of errors or problems occurring, which can have negative impacts on the organization's operations and reputation.

5.4 Program plan lessons learned

General overview	Overall, it is important for a program plan to be well-thought-out, comprehensive, and inclusive of the needs and concerns of all relevant parties to ensure its success.
Lack of clear goals & objectives	A poorly planned program may not have clear and specific goals and objectives, leading to confusion and lack of direction for the team.
Poor stakeholder management	A program plan that does not adequately consider the needs and concerns of key stakeholders can lead to resistance and lack of buy-in.
Insufficient resources	A program plan that does not allocate sufficient resources (e.g., budget, personnel) can lead to delays and problems executing the plan.
Inadequate risk management	A program plan that does not adequately address potential risks and how to mitigate them can lead to unexpected issues and setbacks.
Lack of comms	A program plan that lacks clear communication channels and transparency can lead to misunderstandings and mistrust among team members and stakeholders.

5.5 Change & Comms

Change management and communications are two important aspects of any business transformation initiative. Here are some key considerations for each:

Change management:

- Establishing a clear vision and objectives for the transformation
- Identifying and assessing the impact of the change on different stakeholders
- Developing a plan for implementing the change, including a timeline and budget
- Communicating the change effectively to all stakeholders, including employees, customers, and partners
- Providing support and training to help stakeholders adapt to the change
- Monitoring and measuring the success of the change

Communications:

- Determining the key messages to be communicated about the transformation
- Identifying the most effective channels for communicating those messages (e.g., email, meetings, social media)
- Developing a communications plan that outlines the specific messages to be conveyed at each stage of the transformation
- Ensuring that the right information is delivered to the right stakeholders at the right time
- Monitoring and adjusting the communications plan as needed based on feedback and other factors
- Evaluating the effectiveness of the communications plan after the transformation is complete.

Poor change management and communication can have a number of negative impacts on a business transformation initiative. Some potential impacts include:

- Without proper communication, employees may be resistant to change because they are not fully informed about the reasons for the transformation or how it will affect them. This can lead to low morale and productivity, as well as an increase in turnover.
- Poor change management and communication can increase the risk of project failure, as it can lead to delays, budget overruns, and a lack of buy-in from key stakeholders.

5.5 Change & comms workstream activities

Change vision	Review the vision for change and the reasons for it.
Change resources	Ensure resources with change specialist skills & experience.
Change assessment	Review ASIS and CIA assessment for defined TOBE change.
Change plans	Review change plan with appropriate comms and training.
Change feedback	Review feedback on acceptance of change and change plan.
Change & comms outcome	OCM & comms are proactively actioned & reported

5.5 Change questions

Scope of the change	**What is the scope of the change?**
	A clear understanding of the scope of the change, including what is being changed, who will be impacted, and the timeline for the change is important.
Transformation goals & objectives	**What are the goals and objectives of the change?**
	It is key to have a good understanding of the transformation goals and objectives and how the change will contribute to the overall success of the organization.
Change management plan	**How will the change be implemented?**
	Organizations should have a plan for how the change will be implemented, including who will be responsible for leading the change and what resources will be required.
Change impact	**How will the impact of the change be managed?**
	It is important to consider how the impact of the change will be managed, and how staff will be supported during the transition and how the change will be communicated.
Change metrics	**How will the success of the change be measured?**
	Firms should have a plan for how the success of the change will be measured, including KPIs and other metrics.
Change contingencies	**What contingencies are in place if change has issues?**
	It is important to have contingency plans in place in case the change does not go as planned, including an issue process.

5.5 Comms questions

General overview	Effective comms is key for a transformation initiative success as it helps ensure that all stakeholders are informed.
Stakeholder identification	**Who are the stakeholders?**
	Identify all stakeholders who will be affected by the transformation, and how best to communicate to them.
Information needs	**What information needs to be communicated?**
	Determine what stakeholders need to know about the transformation, and what key messages you want to convey.
Communication methods	**How will information be communicated?**
	Use the most effective channels for delivering your messages (email, meetings, presentations, or newsletters).
Communication frequency	**When will information be communicated?**
	Plan out a timeline for communication that ensures that all stakeholders receive timely and regular updates.
Communication responsibilities	**Who will be responsible for communicating?**
	Designate a person to lead the communication efforts, and ensure that they have the necessary resources and support.
Communication metrics	**How will the effectiveness of comms be measured?**
	Develop metrics to track the success of your communication efforts, such as the level of stakeholder engagement or the number of questions asked.

5.5 Change plan components

General overview	A change management plan is a document that outlines the steps necessary to successfully transition people and organizations from a current state to a desired future state. It is an essential part of any transformation initiative, as it helps the changes be implemented smoothly and efficiently and that people are prepared and able to adapt to the changes.
Change description	A clear and concise description of the change that is being implemented, including its scope, purpose, and benefits.
Change activities	A detailed list of the specific actions and activities that will be required to implement the change, including any necessary training, communication, or process changes.
Timeline	A timeline that outlines the sequence of events and milestones to be used to track progress & measure success.
Budget	A budget that outlines the financial resources that will be required to implement the change, including any necessary investments in new technology or infrastructure.
Risk assessment	A risk assessment that identifies and evaluates potential risks and challenges that may arise during the implementation process, and outlines contingency plans to address them.
Communications plan	A communication plan that outlines how the change will be communicated to staff & key stakeholders.
Training plan	A training plan that outlines the training and support that will be provided to people to help them adapt to the change.
Measurement plan	A measurement plan outlines the metrics used to evaluate change success & the change impact on the business.

5.5 Change impact plan components

Scope	Define the scope of the change impact analysis, including the specific business transformation initiative and the systems, processes, and stakeholders that will be affected.
Objectives	Clearly define the objectives of the change impact analysis, including the specific questions or issues that need to be addressed.
Methodology	Outline the methodology that will be used to conduct the change impact analysis, including any tools or techniques that will be employed.
Data collection	Determine the data that will be needed to conduct the change impact analysis and develop a plan for collecting this data.
Analysis	Define the approach that will be used to analyse the data and identify the potential impacts of the business transformation initiative.
Communications	Develop a plan for communicating the results of the change impact analysis to relevant stakeholders, including any recommendations for addressing potential impacts.
Monitoring and review	Establish a process for monitoring the implementation of the business transformation initiative and reviewing the results of the change impact analysis to ensure that the anticipated impacts are being properly addressed.

5.5 Change training plan components

Objectives	Clearly define the goals and objectives of the training program, including what specific skills or knowledge employees are expected to gain.
Audience	Identify the target audience for the training, including their job roles and any relevant background information.
Content	Develop a curriculum that covers the necessary skills and knowledge required for the transformation. Topics to include such as new technologies, processes, or business strategies.
Delivery	Choose the most appropriate method for delivering the training, such as in-person workshops, online courses, or a combination of both.
Schedule	Determine a schedule for the training that works for both the trainers and the participants.
Evaluation	Develop a system for evaluating the effectiveness of the training (pre- and post-tests, surveys, or focus groups).
Resources	Identify any resources that will be needed for the training, such as materials, software, or equipment.

5.5 Comms plan components

Objectives	Clearly define the goals and objectives of the training plan and how it aligns with the overall transformation initiative.
Target audience	Identify who the training is for and tailor the content and delivery methods to meet their needs and learning styles.
Content	Develop a curriculum that covers the knowledge and skills necessary for the target audience to successfully implement and support the business transformation.
Delivery methods	Choose the most effective methods for delivering the training, such as in-person workshops, online courses, or a combination of both.
Evaluation	Include measures for evaluating the effectiveness of the training (pre- and post-tests, surveys, or focus groups).
Resource allocation	Determine the budget and resources needed to deliver the training, including any necessary materials or technology.
Implementation	Create a detailed plan for implementing the training, including a timeline, milestones, and roles and responsibilities.
Maintenance	Develop a plan for ongoing support and maintenance of the training, including updates to the curriculum as needed.

5.5 Change best practices

Communicate early & frequently	It is important to keep all stakeholders informed about the changes that are being made and the reasons for them. This can help to build support for the transformation and minimize disruption.
Involve employees in the planning process	Engaging employees in the planning process can help to build ownership and buy-in for the changes that are being made. This can be done through focus groups, town hall meetings, and other types of employee involvement.
Clear vision & goals	Having a clear vision and specific, measurable goals can help to guide the transformation and provide a sense of direction for those involved.
Change management team	Designating a dedicated change management team can help to coordinate and oversee the transformation process. This team should have representation from different parts of the organization and should be empowered to make decisions and drive the change process forward.
Resistance to change	It is common for employees to resist change, even if they ultimately believe it is for the best. It is important to anticipate and address this resistance proactively, through open communication and support for employees as they adjust to the changes.
Monitor & adjust change	It is important to continuously monitor the progress of the transformation and make adjustments as needed. This may include gathering feedback from employees, reviewing key performance indicators, and making adjustments to the change plan as necessary.

5.5 Comms best practices

General overview	By following these best practices, you can ensure that all stakeholders are well-informed and engaged in the business transformation process.
Define & communicate goals	Clearly define the goals and objectives of the initiative and communicate them to all stakeholders.
Identify key stakeholders	Identify the key stakeholders and determine the most effective way to communicate with each group.
Create comms plan	Establish a communication plan that outlines the frequency and medium of communication, as well as the specific messages to be conveyed.
Consistent comms	Ensure that all communication is transparent and consistent.
Various comms channels	Use various communication channels, such as email, meetings, and newsletters, to reach all stakeholders.
Open communications	Encourage open and honest communication, and allow for feedback and input from all stakeholders.
Communications responsibility	Assign a team or individual to be responsible for managing and coordinating all communication efforts.
Regular reviews	Regularly review and update the communication plan as needed.

5.5 Change risks

Resistance to change	People may resist change, even if it is ultimately beneficial, because they are comfortable with the status quo or because they are unsure of how the change will impact them.
Communication breakdown	If communication is poor or information is not properly disseminated, employees may become confused or frustrated, leading to decreased morale and productivity.
Lack of resources	Business transformation initiatives often require additional resources, such as funding, personnel, or technology. Change management is a specialist skill and often needs the assistance of an experienced third party. If these resources are not secured, the initiative may be hindered.
Inadequate planning	If the planning process is rushed or inadequate, the transformation initiative may not achieve its desired outcomes or may take longer than expected.
Loss of key personnel	If key personnel leave the organization during the transformation process, it can disrupt the initiative and make it more difficult to achieve success.
Misalignment of goals	If the goals of the transformation initiative are not aligned with the overall goals of the organization, it may be difficult to gain support and achieve success.

5.5 Comms risks

Misunderstandings	Poor communication can lead to misunderstandings about the goals, objectives, and plans of the transformation initiative. This can lead to confusion and misalignment among team members, which can hinder progress.
Decreased motivation	If team members do not feel included in the transformation process or do not understand how it will impact their work, they may become disengaged and less motivated to contribute to the initiative.
Resistance to change	Poor communication can also create resistance to change among team members, as they may feel uncertain about the implications of the transformation and how it will affect them.
Decreased collaboration	Poor communication can lead to a breakdown in collaboration, as team members may be unable to effectively share ideas, information, and resources with one another.
Negative impact on business outcomes	Ultimately, poor communication can have a negative impact on the success of the business transformation initiative, as it can hinder progress and limit the benefits of the initiative

5.5 Change lessons learned

Cleary define the change	It is important to clearly define and communicate the change to all stakeholders. This includes explaining the reason for the change, the benefits it will bring, and how it will be done.
Engage stakeholders	Involving all stakeholders, including staff customers, and external partners, in the change process can help to ensure that the change is successful. This can be done through regular communication, consultation, and collaboration.
Create a sense of ownership	Helping staff and other stakeholders feel ownership of the change can increase their commitment to it. This can be done by involving them in the change process, providing them with training and support, and recognizing their contributions.
Manage resistance	Change can be difficult for people, and it is important to anticipate and manage resistance. This can be done through open and honest communication, addressing concerns and addressing the root causes of resistance.
Ongoing improvement	A culture that supports continuous improvement and adaptability can help organizations to successfully navigate change and remain competitive in the long-term. This can be achieved through leadership, training, and supporting employees in their professional development.

5.5 Comms lessons learned

Misunderstandings & confusion	Lack of clear communication can lead to misunderstandings and confusion among employees, which can hinder progress and create a negative impact on the overall initiative.
Lack of buy-in	Poor communication can also lead to a lack of buy-in and support from employees, which can negatively impact the success of the transformation.
Comms channels	It is important to establish clear communication channels and to make sure that all employees are aware of the changes and their roles in the transformation process.
Honest comms	It is also important to be transparent and open with employees about the reasons for the transformation and to seek their input and feedback.
Regular communications	Regular communication and updates throughout the process can help to ensure that everyone is on the same page and can prevent misunderstandings & miscommunications.

THE WINDS AND WAVES ARE ALWAYS ON THE SIDE OF THE ABLEST NAVIGATORS.

Edward Gibbon

Acknowledgements

One Page Concept: Ken Martin

Source of Royalty Free Quotes (pre-1923):
The GoldenQuotes.Net

3 Magic Publications

Birmingham.

United Kingdom

3 Magic Publications

After an extensive successful career working for some of the best organisations in the world in various countries, I was disheartened to see how many times programs and projects failed from not paying heed to lessons learned and best practices. Even today, how many current programs are being executed without proper assessment, planning or organisational change management, And then organisations are surprised why so many of the programs and projects fail to deliver any business benefits.

I decided to author and to create several Best Practice Books based on my **One Page Magic**™ format on topics such as PMO, Project Management & Business Transformation for leaders to learn from other's experience for project success. When opportunities arise, I collaborate with others to capture their knowledge, experience and best practices to produce additional best practices books.

Other Publications on Amazon

OPM best practices handbooks
- PMO handbook
- Transformation handbook
- Transformational leadership handbook
- CIO handbook
- CTO handbook

One Page Magic series
- PMO magic
- Transformation magic
- PM magic
- Opex magic
- Leader magic
- Agile magic
- Career magic

The OPM Demystified series
- PMO demystified
- PM demystified

The OPM 8-minute series
- CIO/ CTO guide
- DT/ CX guide
- Agile guide
- PMO setup guide
- Live your future guide
- Career guide
- Program planning guide
- Operational excellence guide
- Leadership guide
- Fintech guide
- Disruptive tech guide
- Transformation PMO guide
- PMO governance guide

The Magic Megabook series
- The transformation magic megabook
- The PMO magic megabook

Printed in Great Britain
by Amazon